# DELIGHTING
## IN THE
# TRINITY

To my wife, Helen.
Living in relationship with you has
brought me freedom and joy,
and enriched my humanity.

O Lord, one God, God the Trinity,
whatsoever I have said in these books that comes of thy prompting,
may thy people acknowledge it:
for what I have said that comes only of myself,
I ask of thee and of thy people pardon.

The concluding sentence of Augustine's *On the Trinity*

# Contents

# Chapter 1

# Introduction: Believing in the triune God

*Many of us find the doctrine of the Trinity – that God is three persons sharing one nature – difficult to get our heads round and frankly a bit embarrassing. What is more, we seem to get by without it. But in reality the Trinity is at the heart of all we believe. The Trinity gives shape to Christian truth.*

*Many people claim to believe in god, but have no time for him. That is because their god is remote and uninvolved. The triune God sent his Son into human history so that we could know him as our Father and he sends his Spirit to accompany us in the struggles of life. To find our more about this God is a wonderful adventure.*

Let me begin by explaining how this book came to be written. I was reading the Bible with two friends who are Muslims. Each week they faithfully came to my home and we discussed a passage of Scripture over a cup of tea. Many of their questions were about the Trinity: How can God have a son? How can there be three Gods and one God? The first time these questions came up I thought to myself, "Oh no, they've asked a question about the Trinity. What am I going to say? How can I move the conversation onto different ground?"

## An embarrassing doctrine?

I was embarrassed by the doctrine of the Trinity. The more I thought about it, the more my attitude struck me as crazy. The living God is triune. It is madness to be embarrassed about the Trinity because that means being embarrassed about God! The triune God revealed in the Bible is good news and so the Trinity must be good news. And so I thought on. How is the doctrine of the Trinity good news? This book is my answer to that question.

I have written a number of books. But this book is the one I have enjoyed writing the most. Thinking through the doctrine of the Trinity takes us deeper into the triune God who is the foundation of all reality. This is the God who made us to know him, and who gives meaning and joy to our lives. To explore him is a wonderful adventure. To delight in him is our chief end.

The study of the doctrine of the Trinity readily tips over into worship. We are left with a profound sense of awe as we gaze upon our great God. And such worship leads on to godly living. The root of sin is always idolatry. We turn from the true God to find satisfaction in other things and other ways of life. And so to have our worship of God reignited cuts away at the idolatry in our hearts. "Why spend money on what is not bread, and your labour on what does not satisfy?" says Isaiah. "Listen, listen to me, and eat what is good, and your soul will delight in the richest of fare" (Isaiah 55:2). The triune God is rich fare.

So we should not be embarrassed by the doctrine of the Trinity. We should – and can – love studying it and relish telling others about it. I hope to show that being asked a question about the Trinity is a lovely opportunity to share the heart of our faith.

## An irrelevant doctrine?

Robin Parry says: "For many Christians the Trinity has become something akin to their appendix: it's there, but they're not sure what its function is, they get by in life without it doing very much, and if they had to have it removed they wouldn't be too distressed."[1] Is the doctrine of the Trinity irrelevant? Looking round the church one might think so. In my local Christian bookshop I could not find a single book on the doctrine of the Trinity. So congratulations on finding this one!

Alister McGrath writes: "Most evangelicals do not talk about the Trinity at all." McGrath continues: "The real heartbeat of evangelicalism is in a church Bible study group. If you go there and listen, there will be a lot about Jesus and Jesus' impact on us. But the Trinity is not seen as centrally important; it is seen as difficult."[2] Peter Toon says that, while all major denominations affirm the doctrine of the Trinity, "few of their preachers and teachers actually proclaim this belief in sermons…there is a general feeling that the Trinity is both difficult and unimportant."[3] I recently sorted through about fifty of my theological journals – all self-consciously evangelical. I was looking through the articles, deciding which to keep, when it suddenly occurred to me that not one was on the Trinity. I started looking, but found only one article out of over 400. One reason for this neglect is that evangelicals are people of "the Book" by conviction and activists by nature.[4] They are Bible people with little interest for what might be perceived as extra-biblical speculation with lit-

1. Robin Parry, *Worshipping Trinity: Coming Back to the Heart of Worship* (Paternoster, 2005).
2. Alister McGrath, "Trinitarian Theology" in Mark A. Noll and Ronald F. Thiemann (eds), *Where Shall My Wond'ring Soul Begin: The Landscape of Evangelical Piety and Thought* (Eerdmans, 2000), p. 53.
3. Peter Toon and James D. Spiceland (eds), *One God in Trinity* (Samuel Bagster, 1980), p. xi.
4. D. W. Bebbington, *Evangelicalism in Modern Britain* (Unwin Hyman, 1989), pp. 10–14, and Mark A. Noll, *The Rise of Evangelicalism* (Apollos, 2004), pp. 16–18.

tle relevance to the day-to-day realities of the Christian life.

In reality, however, the Trinity is anything but irrelevant. The doctrine of the Trinity is central to how we know God, how we can be rescued from sin, how we understand the life and mission of the church, and even what it means to be human. Michael Jenson says: "The doctrine of the Trinity underpins our very existence as Christians – it gives a unique shape to the Christian life."[5] There is a trinitarian structure to every part of Christian truth and Christian living. Walter Kasper calls it "the grammar" of salvation.[6]

The Father creates through the Son (Colossians 1:15–17; Hebrews 1:2). God spoke the world into being and the Word he spoke was his Son (John 1:1–3). And the Son continues to be involved in creation, sustaining all things by his powerful word (Hebrews 1:3). God gives life to the first man by breathing "the breath of life" into his nostrils (Genesis 2:7). The word "breath" is the same word as the "Spirit" or "wind" hovering over the waters (Genesis 1:2). The creative Word of God comes on the breath of God. "By the word of the LORD were the heavens made, their starry host by the breath of his mouth" (Psalm 33:6).

In a similar way, the work of salvation reflects the trinitarian activity of God. Throughout the Old Testament, God appears to his people in human form (Joshua 5:13–15; Ezekiel 1:25–28) and his Spirit mediates his presence among his people (Nehemiah 9:20, 30; Isaiah 63:10–14). When Jesus comes, he is sent by the Father (John 6:38–40). He is born of a virgin by the Holy Spirit (Luke 1:34–35). At his baptism the Father speaks

---

5. Michael Jenson, "The Very Practical Doctrine of the Trinity", *The Briefing* 249 (March 2001), p. 11.
6. Walter Kasper, *The God of Jesus Christ* (SCM, 1982), p. 311.

from heaven, commending his Son, and the Spirit descends in the form of a dove (Mark 1:9–11). Jesus conducts his ministry in the power of the Spirit (Matthew 12:28; Luke 4:14; John 3:34) – just as Isaiah had promised (Luke 4:18–19).

On the cross the Father gives his Son to save us (John 3:16). The Son lays down his life for his people in obedience to the Father, but freely of his own accord (John 10:17–18). So we are reconciled to the Father through the death of the Son on our behalf (2 Corinthians 5:19). The Father raises the Son through the Spirit (Romans 1:4; 8:11). The Son is now the mediator between God and humanity (1 Timothy 2:5). The Father sends the Spirit in the name of Jesus (John 14:16–17, 26), and Jesus sends the Spirit from the Father (John 15:26). The Spirit applies the work of the Son to our lives. He brings conviction of sin, righteousness and judgment (John 16:7–11). He opens our eyes to recognise Jesus as Lord (1 Corinthians 12:3). Through the Spirit we are born again (John 3:5–8) and through the Spirit the Father gives us the new life of Christ (Romans 8:11).

So we are saved because of the Father's kindness through rebirth by the Spirit whom he poured out on us through the Son (Titus 3:4–7). Some people look for security in a subjective experience of the Spirit; others in the objective work of Christ. But Christian assurance encompasses both, for it has a threefold basis in trinitarian grace. It is rooted in the electing love of the Father, the finished work of the Son and the present witness of the Spirit. James Torrance says three answers can be given to the question "When did I become a Christian?":

> Firstly, I have been a child of God from all eternity in the heart of the Father. Secondly, I became a child of God when Christ the Son lived, died and rose again for me long ago. Thirdly, I become a child of God when the Holy Spirit – the Spirit of adoption – sealed in my

faith and experience what had been planned from all eternity in the heart of the Father and what was completed once and for all in Jesus Christ. There are three moments but only one act of salvation, just as we believe there are three persons in the Trinity, but only one God.[7]

The structure of prayer mirrors the trinitarian structure of salvation. Although prayer can be offered to the Son and the Spirit, the norm in the New Testament is for prayer to be directed to our Father (Luke 11:1–13). The Son is always the mediator of prayer. We pray in Christ's name for through his death we can draw near to God with confidence (Hebrews 4:14–16; 10:19–22). And the Spirit helps us in the act of praying, enabling us to call on God as our Father and interceding for us in our weakness (Romans 8:14–16, 26–27).[8] Likewise, worship is "our participation through the Spirit in the Son's communion with the Father, in his vicarious life of worship and intercession".[9] Worship is not primarily what we offer to the one God, but the gift of participating in the trinitarian life. Christians offer a priestly "sacrifice of praise" (Hebrews 13:15–16) through Christ's priesthood (Hebrews 2:12; 8:2). Calvin says, "Christ is the great choirmaster who tunes our hearts to sing God's praises."[10]

The trinitarian gospel also leaves its imprint on the community which the gospel brings into being. The church is the people of God (1 Peter 2:9–10); the body of Christ and the bride for which he gave his life (1 Corinthians 12; Ephesians 5:25–27; Revelation 21:2); and the community of the Holy Spirit (2 Corinthians 13:14). We are baptised into the church "in the name of the

7. James B. Torrance, *Worship, Community and the Triune God of Grace* (Paternoster/IVP, 1996), p. 76.
8. On the trinitarian structure of prayer see Tim Chester, *The Message of Prayer* (IVP, 2003), chapters 1–4.
9. James B. Torrance, *Worship, Community and the Triune God of Grace*, p. 15. See also T. F. Torrance, *Theology in Reconstruction* (SCM, 1965), pp. 248–251.
10. Cited in James B. Torrance, *Worship, Community and the Triune God of Grace*, p. 10.

Father and of the Son and of the Holy Spirit" (Matthew 28:19). The church is the place where God lives by his Spirit (Ephesians 2:22). Christ gives gifts to his people through the Spirit (1 Corinthians 12:8–11; Ephesians 4:7–13). God works in us through his Spirit that we might serve the Lord Jesus Christ (1 Corinthians 12:4–6).

Paul says: "Through [Christ] we both have access to the Father by one Spirit" (Ephesians 2:18). Everywhere we look, we find this trinitarian structure to Christian truth and Christian living. "We live, move and have our being," says Robert Letham, "in a pervasively trinitarian atmosphere." [11] The Son works for us and the Spirit works in us in fulfilment of the Father's will. "[We] have been chosen," says Peter, "according to the foreknowledge of God the Father, through the sanctifying work of the Spirit, for obedience to Jesus Christ and sprinkling by his blood" (1 Peter 1:2). If we say the Trinity is too difficult to bother with then we are saying that God is too difficult to bother with, for "Trinity is the Christian name for God." [12]

If you really want to understand a culture, then you have to understand the language. It is no good visiting a country, looking at its historic sites, reading translations of its literature, finding out its history. That is why maintaining indigenous languages is so important to preserving cultural identity. The same is true of the Christian faith. To understand it fully you must learn its language, and its language is the Trinity. The Trinity is the language in which Christian truth is spoken. It gives shape to the truth. The Trinity is not peripheral, let alone optional. It is the marvellous, wonderful heart of our faith.

---

11. Robert Letham, "The Trinity – Yesterday, Today and the Future", *Themelios* 28:1 (Autumn 2002), p. 32.
12. Karl Barth, cited in Gordon D. Fee, *The First Epistle to the Corinthians*, NICNT (Eerdmans, 1987), p. 586.

## An unbelievable doctrine?

I love mathematical puzzles and patterns. Do you know what you get if you key 1.2345678 into a calculator and hit the square root button? (You will have to try it if you want to find out!) For many people the Trinity is a mathematical trick; a rather improbable attempt to make 1 + 1 + 1 = 1. It is certainly true that the triune nature of God pushes our knowledge and imagination to the limits and beyond. But then, as Augustine said, "If you can understand it, it's not God."[13]

Roger Nicole says: "It is important to recognise that the doctrine of the Trinity is a mystery. It is not, however, an absurdity, as some people have viewed it. Specifically, it is not asserted that God is one in the same respect in which he is three."[14] We are not making three equal one. We are saying that three divine persons share one divine nature. God's oneness "is not a mathematical oneness... but a oneness consisting in the inseparable relation of Father, Son and Spirit, the [persons]. The doctrine of the Trinity has... nothing to do with attempting a mathematical innovation, apparently contradictory."[15] We need not fear the doctrine of the Trinity.

Many of the words we use for "knowing" are aggressive terms. We *grasp* ideas or *get hold* of them. We *seize* them and *grapple* with them. We try to *get a handle on* them and *come to terms* with them. We *catch, capture* and *apprehend* an idea. They are all words that imply control. After all, knowledge is power. But God cannot be known in this way. We cannot seize or grasp God. He is beyond our control. Our problem is not simply lack of information. Our problem is that the "subject" of our investiga-

---

13. Cited in Alister McGrath, *Understanding the Trinity* (Kingsway, 1987), p. 9.
14. Roger Nicole, "The Meaning of the Trinity" in Peter Toon and James D. Spiceland (eds), *One God in Trinity* (Samuel Bagster, 1980), p. 4.
15. Colin Gunton, *The Promise of Trinitarian Theology* (T&T Clark, 1991), pp. 9–10.

tion is far beyond our comprehension and control. So we cannot expect to understand the triune God. We cannot grasp God or get hold of him any more than we can grasp a fistful of water.

But, though we cannot know God fully, we can know him truly. If we read a biography of a person our knowledge of them will be limited. Even with the current fashion for psychological analysis in biographies, we will not comprehend the inner life of the person. But we can still know something true about that person. We may know many of the facts of their life and gain an accurate, albeit incomplete, sense of their character. We might even be able to predict how they would react in certain situations. In the same way, we cannot fully comprehend the inner life of God, but we can know something true about his actions and character. And there is an importance difference between the biography and our knowledge of God. We not only read about God in the Bible, we can also know him personally. We experience him dwelling within us. We can have a relationship with him. Colin Gunton concludes: "Because we are established in our being in the Trinity, we are enabled to think *from*, and, with careful qualification, *about* the triune being of God."[16] In other words, when we consider the Trinity we are not reflecting on something wholly alien to us, but something that is reflected in our experience.

Less than ten per cent of the UK population go to church regularly, yet according to a 2003 ICM poll two-thirds believe in god. Some people find this surprising. Others see it as an optimistic sign. But the reality is that these people do not believe in God – not the true God. They believe perhaps in a god who made the world and now leaves us to its own devices or an all-pervading reality like "the force" in the *Star Wars* movies. But they do

16. Colin Gunton, *The Promise of Trinitarian Theology*, p. 6.

not believe in "the God and Father of our Lord Jesus Christ" (Romans 15:6). We cannot talk about belief in God without asking which god we believe in. So many of the people who claim to believe in god do not believe in God – not the God who truly exists and has truly revealed himself in Jesus Christ.

This also means that the god many people have rejected is not the true God. They have rejected another god – an idol of human making. Tom Wright says: "The 'God' the great majority of people believe in is, pretty certainly, the Deist god...distant, remote, and uncaring... It's not surprising that people who believe in the existence of that sort of god don't go to church except now and then. It's hardly worth getting out of bed for a god like that." [17] They are not involved with god because their god is not involved with them. But the Christian message is the good news that God is involved. The Father sent his Son into the pain and confusion of human history to reconcile us to himself and now he gives his Spirit to accompany us in the struggles of life. By telling the story of the triune God we invite people to know the God who both rules the world and has come close to us, welcoming us into his family. And that *is* a God worth getting out of bed for!

A member of my church was looking at the Trinity with me, working through much of the material in this book. At the end he wrote to me:

> Before I looked at the Trinity I was a little bit embarrassed about God. Without the Trinity God is incomprehensible. I had bits about God; now I have a whole. It's beautiful, stunning. Before I had a far-off God. Now I want to draw near to him. He's more appealing to me. I feel I've got a story to tell about God which is convincing. I have a story in the Trinity that connects with the world.

---

17. Tom Wright, *What Saint Paul Really Said* (Lion, 1997), pp. 161–162.

# PART ONE
# Biblical foundations

# Chapter 2

# The unity of God in the Bible

*At the heart of Israelite faith was the so-called "Shema": "The LORD our God, the LORD is one." It affirms the uniqueness and oneness of God as well as his identity as the God of Israel. The New Testament weaves Jesus into the Shema, identifying him as the LORD without compromising the oneness of God. God is one, undivided and singular.*

*Many of us sometimes function as if God consists of three separate beings. Some people separate Word and Spirit, others argue that God can be known apart from Jesus. But God is one and undivided. The one, undivided God demands undivided love and allegiance. Worshipping God involves forsaking the worship of idols in whatever form they come.*

On one occasion a teacher of the law asked Jesus: "Which commandment is the most important of all?" (Mark 12:28, ESV). Jesus answered:

> The most important is, "Hear, O Israel: The Lord our God, the Lord is one. And you shall love the Lord your God with all your heart and with all your soul and with all your mind and with all your strength." The second is this: "You shall love your neighbour as yourself." There is no other commandment greater than these. (Mark 12:29–31, ESV)

Jesus begins his response with a quotation from Deuteronomy 6:4. He points in the first place not to an ethical command, but to a statement of Israelite belief – perhaps the greatest statement of Israelite belief: "The LORD our God, the LORD is one."

## The Shema: The LORD our God, the LORD is one

### The uniqueness of God

These words are known as the "Shema" after the opening words in Hebrew. In Hebrew they consist of just four words: Yahweh our-God Yahweh one (the word 'is' is implicit).[1]

The first thing the Shema affirms is the uniqueness of God. Israelite faith is often expressed in "henotheistic" terms. Henotheism is the belief that there are other gods, but only one God is to be worshipped. The surrounding nations worshipped other gods and Israel is called to turn from such gods to worship Yahweh alone. The first commandment is phrased in this sort of way: "You shall have no other gods before me" (Deuteronomy 5:7). But the talk of other gods is ultimately rhetorical. They exist because they are worshipped and named, but they do not truly exist. The LORD alone is God (1 Kings 8:60). The Psalmist says: "all the gods of the nations are idols, but the LORD made the heavens" (Psalm 96:5).

The story of creation in Genesis Chapter 1 is written as a polemic against polytheism. The creation stories of the nations around Israel involved a pantheon of gods, often in conflict with one another. But in Genesis God is the only agent. He alone is "in the beginning" and he alone creates through his word. God alone is to be worshipped because he alone is the Sovereign Creator.

> For this is what the LORD says –
> he who created the heavens, he is God;
> he who fashioned and made the earth, he founded it...
> he says: "I am the LORD, and there is no other." (Isaiah 45:18)

---

1. See J. G. McConville, *Deuteronomy*, AOTC (Apollos, 2002), pp. 140–141.

> We are bringing you good news, telling you to turn from these
> worthless things to the living God, who made heaven and earth
> and sea and everything in them. (Acts 14:15)

The monotheism of Israel was further reinforced by stories of pagans who come to acknowledge Yahweh as the
one true God (2 Kings 5; Daniel 2 – 4). When the
Philistines bring the ark into the temple of Dagon, it is
the idol of Dagon who falls before the ark and has to be
propped up again (1 Samuel 5:1–5). Before the true God
all other idols are revealed in their impotence.

## The oneness of God

But the Shema is affirming more than the uniqueness of
God. As we have seen, the LORD alone is God – there is no
other (Deuteronomy 4:35, 39). But the words "alone" and
"one" are not the same in Hebrew, and in the Shema
Moses uses the word for "one". Moses is affirming the singularity of Yahweh. Yahweh is not only unique – he is
also one. Other religions of the time used divine names
collectively. Baal was a Canaanite god, but the term was
used of a variety of deities. The gods of Canaan took mul-
tiple forms. In contrast, as Chris Wright puts it, "Yahweh
is not the brand name of a cosmic corporation."[2] "There
is only one Starbucks," someone might say, and we
would know what they meant. Starbucks is one brand
with a common identity. But in reality there are lots of
Starbucks' coffee shops – too many for some people's lik-
ing! When the Shema says Yahweh is one, it is not saying
God is one in the sense that there is only one Starbucks.
Yahweh is not a franchise with many local realities. He is
one.

Moreover, because God is one, he acts with integrity
and consistency. He is not, as it were, double-minded or

---

2. Chris Wright, *Deuteronomy*, NIBC (Hendrickson/Paternoster, 1996), p. 96.

two-faced. "I thought I said you couldn't do that." "But Dad said it was okay." I guess most parents have had an exchange like this, probably many times. When my wife or I told our girls they could not do something, they often went to ask the other, hoping for a positive reply. We had to learn pretty quickly to check what the other parent had said before we responded to our daughters. It is the same with discipline. We try to give similar punishments for similar offences. In other words, we try to speak to our children "with one voice". Of course, we do not always succeed. One of us says "No", the other says "Yes". But God always speaks with one voice. Father, Son and Spirit speak with one voice because they are one. God's words are always consistent. Yahweh has a unity of will and a constancy of character.

### The identity of God

But we are not finished with the Shema yet. It not only affirms that there is one God and that God is one. It says that this God is Yahweh. "Yahweh our God, Yahweh is one." Yahweh is usually rendered as "the LORD" in English translations. It is the name God revealed to Moses. It is not a generic term for deity, but the personal name of God. I am a man called Tim. He is God called Yahweh.

The background to the name "Yahweh" is found in Moses' encounter with God at the burning bush. When Moses asks God's name, God replies: "I AM WHO I AM. This is what you are to say to the Israelites: 'I AM has sent me to you'" (Exodus 3:13–14). Grammatically the term "Yahweh" is probably related to the verb "to be" so that it expresses God's eternal sovereignty. He is "the Lord". But Yahweh is also the covenant name of God. It is the name by which God revealed himself to his people. It is the name which associates him with his promise to Abraham (Exodus 3:15).

So the one God is not known by many names. He has revealed himself as Yahweh. He is known through his involvement with Israel. The Shema is not simply a call to believe in one God. It is saying that the one God has revealed himself uniquely in the history of Israel. It is common today for people to say there is one God and that he is known by many names. Muslims call him Allah, Buddhists call him Buddha, Hindus call him Krishna or other names and Christians call him Jesus. There is a school of thought that says that there is a divine reality at the centre of all things. All religions point to this reality, but the names they use are all penultimate. The ultimate reality is unnamed and ultimately unknowable. The Shema refuses to let biblical religion be fitted into such a scheme. The ultimate divine reality is personal and named. He is Yahweh, revealed in the promises of the Bible and in its story of salvation. Chris Wright says:

> It is vital to see that in Old Testament terms, it is Yahweh who defines what monotheism means, not a concept of monotheism that defines how Yahweh should be understood… [The Shema's] majestic declaration of a monotheism defined by the history-laden, character-rich, covenant-related, dynamic personhood of "Yahweh our God", shows that the abstract and definitionally undefinable "being" of religious pluralism is really a monism without meaning or message.[3]

## The Shema and Jesus: There is one God, the Father, and one Lord, Jesus Christ

In 1 Corinthians 8:6 Paul says: "For us there is one God, the Father, from whom are all things and for whom we exist, and one Lord, Jesus Christ, through whom are all things and through whom we exist" (1 Corinthians 8:6,

---

3.  Chris Wright, *Deuteronomy*, p. 96.

ESV). When you take out the statements about "from whom, for whom and through whom" you are left with: "There is one God, the Father...and one Lord, Jesus Christ..." It is clearly a reworking of the Shema. In verse four of the same chapter Paul has already said: "There is no God but one." But woven into Paul's reworking of the Shema is Jesus Christ.

| The LORD our God | the LORD is one | (Deuteronomy 6:4) |
| one God, the Father | one Lord, Jesus Christ | (1 Corinthians 8:6) |

Most of the meat sold in Corinth would have been first offered to idols. Temples doubled as restaurants. Imagine you were invited for a meal with your neighbours. Meat is on the menu and you know it has been offered to idols. What should you do? You do not want to give offence, but should you associate with idolatry in this way? Some in Corinth argued that since idols are nothing eating the meat offered to them was okay. Others argued that idolatry involved false worship – maybe even demonic in origin – so Christians should not associate with such practices or give credence to such beliefs. In responding to this issue Paul says:

> So then, about eating food sacrificed to idols: We know that an idol is nothing at all in the world and that there is no God but one. For even if there are so-called gods, whether in heaven or on earth (as indeed there are many "gods" and many "lords"), yet for us there is but one God, the Father, from whom all things came and for whom we live; and there is but one Lord, Jesus Christ, through whom all things came and through whom we live. (1 Corinthians 8:4–6)

Paul goes on to talk about how Christians should treat graciously those whose conscience does not allow them to eat meat offered to idols. But notice that his argument in verses 4–6 depends on classic Jewish monotheism. This is why he employs the classic statement of Jewish monotheism – the Shema. We can eat meat offered to idols because idols have no real existence. We know idols have no real existence because God is one. And yet it is at this point that Paul interweaves Jesus Christ. Jesus Christ is that one God.

> The whole argument of the chapter hinges precisely on [Paul] being a Jewish-style monotheist, over against pagan polytheism; and, as the lynchpin of the argument, he has quoted the most central and holy confession of that monotheism and has placed Jesus firmly in the middle of it. Lots of Pauline scholars have tried to edge their way round this one, but it can't be done… This verse is one of the mostly genuinely revolutionary bits of theology ever written.[4]

To say as Paul does that Jesus is the Lord is to claim that he is God, for the one Lord of Deuteronomy Chapter 6 is Yahweh. "Paul rewrites the Shema to include both God and Jesus in the unique divine identity."[5] But Jesus is not a second god. He is the one God with the Father. The divinity of Jesus compromises neither the uniqueness, nor the singularity of God. The Father is God and Jesus is God and, as we shall see, the Spirit is God, but God is still one (see also Matthew 23:9; Mark 10:18; 12:29; John 5:44; 17:3; Romans 3:30; 16:27; 1 Corinthians 8:4–6; Galatians 3:20; Ephesians 4:6; 1 Timothy 1:17; 2:5; James 2:19; 4:12; Jude 25).

> One of the most striking things about Pauline Christology – Paul's statement about Jesus – is this: at the very moment when he is giving Jesus the highest titles and honours, he is also emphasising that he, Paul, is a good Jewish-style monotheist. Faced with this evidence, we either have to conclude that Paul was really a very muddled theologian indeed, or that he intended to say, as clearly as was

4. Tom Wright, *What Saint Paul Really Said* (Lion, 1997), pp. 66–67.
5. Richard Bauckham, "Biblical Theology and the Problems of Monotheism" in Craig Bartholomew, Mary Healy, Karl Möller and Robin Parry (eds), *Out of Egypt: Biblical Theology and Biblical Interpretation* (Paternoster/Zondervan, 2004/05).

open to him, that when he put Jesus and God in the same bracket he was not intending that Jesus was seen as somehow absorbed into the being of the one God, without remainder. He was inviting his readers to see Jesus as retaining his full identity as the man Jesus of Nazareth, but within the inner being of one God, the God of Jewish monotheism.[6]

God has one essence or nature. However we conceive of the threeness of God, we cannot do so in a way that compromises the oneness of his being. The Nicene Creed says Jesus is "of one Being with the Father". There is not one God divided into three parts like a chocolate orange. God is one, undivided and singular.

Few people today call themselves "tritheists" – someone who believes in three gods. But in practice, for many of us, the threeness of God eclipses the oneness of God. We conceive of the Father, Son and Spirit as separate beings. Wayne Grudem says: "Many evangelicals today unintentionally tend towards tritheistic views of the Trinity, recognising the distinct personhood of the Father, the Son, and the Holy Spirit, but seldom being aware of the unity of God as one undivided being."[7]

One consequence of this is that we find ourselves focusing on one person of the Trinity to the exclusion of the others. For example, we create a dichotomy between the Word and the Spirit. Some people emphasise the Spirit while others emphasise the Word. Or we say that we need a balance between the two. But to talk of balance assumes they are different things to be held in tension. In reality the testimony to Jesus of the prophets and apostles that we have recorded in the Bible is the work of the Spirit. The Spirit reveals the things of Christ – those things which Christ himself receives from the Father (John 16:13–15). The Spirit is "the Spirit of Christ"

---

6. Tom Wright, *What Saint Paul Really Said*, p. 65.
7. Wayne Grudem, *Systematic Theology* (Zondervan/IVP, 1994), p. 248.

(Romans 8:9). The Spirit is the means by which Christ is present with his people. The word of God is the Spirit-breathed word (2 Timothy 3:16). The Father reveals himself in the Son by the Spirit. So we cannot have a time of "ministry" after the sermon as if the Spirit's work can be separated from the Word of God. We cannot talk of the Spirit's work apart from the Word of God, nor can we think of the Word of God apart from the work of the Spirit. Yahweh speaks with one voice.

Another form this tendency to tritheism takes concerns our view of other religions. Some people suggest that non-Christians can genuinely know God apart from Jesus – an idea sometimes called "anonymous Christianity". But the unity of the Trinity means we cannot know God without Jesus. God cannot be divided so that one person of the Trinity can be known apart from the others.

## The Shema among the nations

The Shema is not an abstract statement of philosophical enquiry. It is a defiant statement with radical consequences. In its original context in Deuteronomy 6 it forms the first half of a sentence which continues: "Love the LORD your God with all your heart and with all your soul and with all your strength" (Deuteronomy 6:5). The undivided God of the Shema should be loved with an undivided love. This is how Jesus uses the Shema in response to the question of the teacher of the law in Mark 12. The teacher of the law wants to prioritise his obedience. He wants to know what he should concentrate on. "If I can fulfil the most important commandment," he thinks to himself, "then maybe I needn't worry so much about some of the others." But, replies Jesus, "the LORD our God, the LORD is one" and therefore no one and nothing can rightfully share the love that is due to him. Our love for our neighbour which Jesus ties together with the command to love God is not a second love, but one of the ways in which we express our love for God. We love God as, in obedience to him, we love those made in his image. Our obedience cannot be prioritised. It must be total.

The Shema is a truth affirmed in the context of competing untruths. It is a command stated in the context of competing allegiances. Time and again it is restated in the context of the nations. In Isaiah 44:6 we read: "This is what the LORD says – Israel's King and Redeemer, the LORD Almighty: I am the first and I am the last; apart from me there is no God." In contrast, says Isaiah, "all who fashion idols are nothing, and the things they delight in do not profit" (Isaiah 44:9, ESV). An idol we can hold in our hands is a lie, for a god we can grasp is no god (see also Isaiah 46:5–13).

In Isaiah 45 we read:

> I am the LORD, and there is no other;
> apart from me there is no God.
> I will strengthen you, though you have not acknowledged me,
> so that from the rising of the sun to the place of its setting
> men may know there is none besides me.
> I am the LORD, and there is no other. (Isaiah 45:5–6)

Once again we have a reworking of the Shema and once again it is stated in the context of the nations. Isaiah writes about one whom God equips even though he does not acknowledge God. This is Cyrus – the king of the Persians (45:1). After Israel had spent 70 years in exile in Babylon, God sent Cyrus to defeat the Babylonians and liberate his people. Though Cyrus does not acknowledge God, he is under God's control. Because God is the one God, he is the God of all nations. All peoples are under his sovereignty – whether they acknowledge him or not.

When I was younger I used to go trekking in the mountains. At night alone in my tent I would sometimes hear noises or see shadows and think something threatening was outside. On one occasion this was true and I found a family of rats trying to share my tent! But most of the time there was nothing. The mad axe-man or angry landowner were fictions, but the impact on me was real enough. The sweat on my brow, the tension in my limbs, the beating of my heart were all real.

The Bible reflects a tension between the non-reality and the reality of other gods. Other gods have no existence, but they are a reality in people's experience. They are named and worshipped by people. They can inhabit, and even control, a person's mind. They are a real threat to God's people. They may take the form of a statue, but they may be money, possessions, sex, pleasure – created things to which we assign the hopes and devotion we should only truly give to God. Idolatry is treating created things as though they were a god (Romans 1:25). Sometimes this is the projection of a sinful mind; sometimes it is the construct of human society that has turned from God. Warning Christians not to take part in non-Christian worship Paul says, "the sacrifices of pagans are offered to demons, not to God, and I do not want you to be participants with demons" (1 Corinthians 10:20). We should not think here of strange occult practices, still less of fork-tailed demons inhabiting idols. Satan is the father of lies. He persuades individuals and societies to worship what is created. It is in this sense that idolatry is demonic. What is created is not God, nor does it give true fulfilment or deliver us from the judgment of God.

We used to live a couple of doors away from someone who worshipped his car. Every Sunday morning, as we set out to walk to the gathering of our church, we would see him kneeling to wash the wheels with a toothbrush. As we joined others in worshipping the living God, he was prostrate before his god. Career, income, financial security, our house, our hobby, sex – we can give our lives to any of these things.

So our worship is a subversive act. It is like singing the national anthem of France in occupied France during the Second World War. We relativise other claims. By giving our allegiance to God, we are withholding it from the empires and ideologies of the world. In our corporate worship we call one another back *to* worship of the true God and *away* from the worship of other gods. As we affirm the worth of God together in song, as we express together our dependence on him in prayer, as we accept one another as those whose identity is found in Christ – in all these ways we call one another back to the worship of the true God. We rescue one another from the subtle influence of the empty and destructive idolatries of this world. We give our undivided love and allegiance to the one, undivided God.

On the day God comes, says the prophet Zechariah: "The LORD will be king over the whole earth. On that day there will be one LORD, and his name the only name" (Zechariah 14:9). On that day the gods that are no-gods will be no more. Today they really exist through the lies of Satan and in the minds of their adherents. But on that day no other god will be named, nor will people say that the one God can be worshipped through different names. Instead "at the name of Jesus every knee should bow, in heaven and on earth and under the earth, and every tongue confess that Jesus Christ is Lord, to the glory of God the Father" (Philippians 2:10–11). The one God is known through Jesus Christ. Paul is quoting from Isaiah 45. Isaiah reworks the Shema not simply as a polemic against idolatry, but as the hope of the nations and the promise of God's ultimate glory.

> Turn to me and be saved,
> all you ends of the earth;
> for I am God, and there is no other.
> By myself I have sworn, my mouth has uttered in all integrity
> a word that will not be revoked:
> Before me every knee will bow;
> by me every tongue will swear. (Isaiah 45:22–23)

That message is as relevant as it ever was. Few of us bow down to idols in the form of statues. But, as Calvin said, our hearts are "idol-making factories". Ezekiel says the real problem are the "idols in their hearts" (Ezekiel 14:1–11). In Romans Paul says:

> Therefore God gave them up in the lusts of their hearts to impurity, to the dishonouring of their bodies among themselves, because they exchanged the truth about God for a lie and worshipped and served the creature rather than the Creator, who is blessed forever! Amen. (Romans 1.24–25, ESV)

Paul goes on to give a list of corrupt and destructive behaviours. This is what we see in our lives and the lives of other people – we see behaviour. But Paul says that such behaviour stems from "the lusts of the heart". Jesus says the same thing when he says that our evil actions come from within; from the heart (Mark 7:21–23). If I lose my temper I may say, "I was provoked." And indeed I may have been provoked, but my anger came from within my heart. Sometimes when my children are naughty, I respond with calm and measured discipline. But sometimes I lose my temper. Do I lose my temper because my children are naughty? In one sense the answer is "Yes", but that does not explain why I lose my temper instead of responding calmly. The truth is that I lose my temper because my children are disrupting my plans for a quiet sit down or preventing me getting some-where on time. I want to be in control. I want to be "god" of my life. And if my children get in the way then I lose it. It is the sinful desires of my heart that cause me to react with anger instead of patience. If some trial in our lives causes us to sin we cannot blame God, says James. Sinful behaviour arises when our reactions are governed by our inner desires (James 1:13–15).

But, says Paul in Romans, the sinful desires of our hearts are themselves the result of exchanging the truth about God for a lie and exchanging the worship of God for idols. Idolatry and lies about God lead to sinful desires which lead in turn to sinful behaviour. The problem is that we often focus on changing the sinful behaviour through self-discipline. But if we ignore the underlying idolatries and lies which shape our hearts then rules for behaviour will not work (Colossians 2:20–23).

Let's suppose I have a problem with my temper. Put me under pressure and I blow; I lose it; I fly off the handle. What would you say to me? Count to ten? Bite your tongue? It is good advice, but on its own it will not bring lasting change to my behaviour. We need to think about what drives my temper. Maybe I need to feel in control and temper is how I exert control on a situation. If so, then I need to be reminded that God is sovereign and he rules in love. Or maybe I feel insecure. If someone in my team at work fails then I worry what others will think of me and so I blow. If so, then I need to be reminded that God in Christ accepts me through his grace. I do not need to justify myself because God has justified me. I do not need to fear others because God is the one I should fear. In both cases I have made an idol of myself. I want to control my world. I want to be in charge. But God is one. There is no place for other gods – especially not one like me!

Idolatry is not a relic of the past. It is alive and well in your heart and mine. It is what drives the lusts of our heart and our destructive behaviour. But God is one. He will not share his glory with another. And worshipping the one God is freedom. Believing the truth about God is what sets us free from the destructive behaviours that enslave us (John 8:31–38). Knowing and serving the one God will liberate me from my temper, my insecurity, my addiction or my depression. The call of Isaiah is as relevant today as ever it was: "Turn to me and be saved, all you ends of the earth; for I am God, and there is no other" (Isaiah 45:22).

# Chapter 3

# The plurality of God in the Bible

*There are signs in the Old Testament that the one God is also in some sense plural. But the coming of Jesus illuminates the trinitarian nature of God. Jesus is clearly a man, but his actions and his words as well as the testimony and worship of the first Christians show he is also divine. The Spirit is identified as God, but also identified as a person who is different from the Father and the Son. So all the ingredients of trinitarianism are in the Bible. The doctrine of the Trinity developed as a way of summarising what we discover in the story of salvation.*

The Bible is not a theological treatise. You cannot look under "G" to find out about God. It is a story: the story of salvation. The doctrine of the Trinity does not start life as a philosophical statement, but as a way of summarising what we discover in the story of salvation.

## The plural God in the Old Testament

The Hebrew word most commonly used for "God" is *Elohim*. It is a plural form. It could imply a plural of quantity or intensity (like the words for "waters" and "heavens"). But Elohim is used with the singular form of a verb. God is both plural and singular. Though on its own this is not decisive, viewed in the light of the whole biblical witness its use is striking. We also find plural pronouns (us, our) and verbs being used of God:

> Then God said, "Let *us* make man in *our* image, in *our* likeness." (Genesis 1:26, my emphasis)

> And the LORD God said, "The man has now become like one of *us*, knowing good and evil." (Genesis 3:22, my emphasis)

> The LORD said… "Come, *let us* go down and confuse their language." (Genesis 11:6–7, my emphasis)

> Then I heard the voice of the LORD saying, "Whom shall I send? And who will go for *us*?" (Isaiah 6:8, my emphasis)

God himself speaks and instead of saying "*I* will", he says "Let *us*". In Genesis Chapter 1 God creates through his Word and then addresses that Word to himself. It suggests a conversation *within* God, revealing a God who is plural and communal. This divine plural has been interpreted as an address to creation or the heavenly court, but it conveys more than information – it suggests collaboration. It has been seen as a kind of royal "we", but this is anachronistic. It could be an expression of self-deliberation, but there are no parallels for this in a plural form.[1] Henri Blocher concludes: "God addresses himself, but this he can do only because he has a Spirit who is both one with him and distinct from him at the same time. Here are the first glimmerings of a trinitarian revelation."[2]

## Seeing the unseen God

The Old Testament is clear that no one may see God and live. Yet throughout people do see God. The angel of the LORD is distinguished from God. He speaks of God as an other (Genesis 18:14; Judges 6:12; 13:8–9, 16). Yet he is also identified with God (Genesis 16:13; 18:1; 22:11–12; Exodus 3:2–4; Judges 2:1; 6:11–14). When Jacob wrestles

---

1. See Henri Blocher, *In the Beginning* (IVP, 1984), pp. 79–97 and David Clines, "The Image of God in Man", *Tyndale Bulletin* 19 (1968), pp. 53–103 for a discussion of the plural *Let us*.
2. Henri Blocher, *In the Beginning*, p. 84.

with the angel he realises he has wrestled with God himself. "Jacob called the place Peniel, saying, 'It is because I saw God face to face, and yet my life was spared'" (Genesis 32:30). Jacob recognises that he ought to have died because to see God is to be consumed and yet he has encountered God (see also Judges 6:22–23; 13:22–23). Moses felt the same tension at the burning bush. "Moses hid his face, because he was afraid to look at God" (Exodus 3:6). Moses knew that he could not see God and live, but he does live. Moreover God promises that "I will be with you" (Exodus 3:12). God is differentiated from God.

## The Wisdom of God
Wisdom is seen in the Old Testament as an attribute of God, but in Proverbs it is personified – a process that continues in inter testamental Judaism (see Wisdom 7:24–26 and Ecclesiasticus 24:1–5). In Proverbs 8:22–31 Wisdom pre-exists the universe. "The LORD brought me forth as the first of his works, before his deeds of old; I was appointed from eternity, from the beginning, before the world began" (Proverbs 8:22–23). Moreover, she is the agent by which God creates, "the craftsman at his side" (Proverbs 8:30–31). The allusions to Proverbs 8 in the New Testament (Colossians 1:15–17; 2:3; Revelation 3:14) suggest that this personification of Wisdom, "far from overshooting the literal truth, was a preparation for its full statement, since the agent of creation was no mere activity of God, but the Son".[3]

## The Spirit of God
The Spirit or Breath of God is also differentiated from God (Genesis 1:2; Numbers 11:25; Psalm 104:30). But the Spirit also describes the agency of God (Isaiah 40:7;

---

3. Derek Kidner, *Proverbs*, TOTC (IVP, 1964), p. 79.

Zechariah 4:6). The Spirit is that by which God enables people to act in extraordinary ways (Genesis 41:38; Exodus 31:3; 35:31; Numbers 11:25; Deuteronomy 34:9; Isaiah 11:2; 42:1; 61:1). The Spirit is synonymous with the presence of God (Psalm 139:7). In future days God will give his Spirit to his people (Isaiah 44:3; Ezekiel 36:26–27; 37:14; Joel 2:28–29). We find both differentiation and identification. Again "Spirit" and "Breath" might be metaphorical personifications of God's power or God's presence. But looking back with trinitarian eyes we can see the third person of the Trinity alive and well in the Old Testament. We can also ask whether there is a better way of making sense of the Spirit's differentiation from, and identification with, God than that provided by the doctrine of the Trinity.

## The Shema

In Chapter 2 we looked at the central confession of Israel, the Shema: "The Lord our God, the Lord is one" (Deuteronomy 6:4). What are we to make of the suggestions of divine plurality in the light of this affirmation of the oneness of God? The Hebrew word for "one" in the Shema is the same word which is used for a man and woman becoming "one flesh" (Genesis 2:24). Marriage involves a unity which contains plurality. So the Shema need not deny plurality within God. But neither is there a plurality of gods. Whatever plurality there may be and whatever form it may take, there is still one God.

The evidence for the plurality of God is striking, but not decisive. It becomes compelling when we read it from a trinitarian perspective. Yet this Christian reading of the Old Testament is the proper one.[4] We must read the Old Testament on its own terms. We cannot disregard the

---

4. On reading the Old Testament from a Christian perspective, see Tim Chester, *From Creation to New Creation: Understanding the Bible Story* (Paternoster, 2003).

intention of the biblical authors, still less can we read into it what we like. But Jesus Christ, the Word of God, provides the definitive hermeneutic of the Old Testament. He describes himself as the one to whom the Old Testament points (Luke 24:25–27, 44–47; John 5:39–40). The Old Testament explains who Jesus is and his coming explains the meaning of the Old Testament. This is not an alien hermeneutic imposed on the text. The Old Testament itself expects a fulfilment and amplification beyond itself in the coming of God's kingdom and God's messiah. The coming of Jesus is that event. He is the ulti-mate revelation of God. He brings the intimations of divine plurality into sharp focus. We should not anachro-nistically suppose that the Old Testament saints were Trinitarians, for something new has taken place with the incarnation of the Son and the coming of the Spirit. But we may suppose that they had intimations of the plural-ity of God for the evidence is there in the record they left.

From earliest times the Patristic, medieval and Reformation theologians identified the divine appearances in the Old Testament with the second person of the Trinity. The Son's role as the revelation of God comes to a climax when he was implanted in Mary's womb by the Spirit, but it did not begin there. Benjamin Warfield writes:

> The Old Testament may be likened to a chamber richly furnished but dimly lighted; the introduction of light brings into it nothing which was not in it before; but it brings out into clearer view much of what is in it but was only dimly or even not at all perceived before. The mystery of the Trinity is not revealed in the Old Testament; but the mystery of the Trinity underlies the Old Testament revelation, and here and there almost comes into view. Thus the Old Testament revelation of God is not corrected by the fuller revelation which follows it, but only perfected, extended and enlarged.[5]

5. Benjamin B. Warfield, "The Biblical Doctrine of the Trinity", *Biblical and Theological Studies* (P&R, 1968), p. 30.

## The humanity of Jesus

In recent years the divinity of Christ has been questioned. It is perhaps a sign of our human-centredness that the humanity of Jesus can be taken for granted. But it is not always the case. I was studying Mark's Gospel with a Chinese student who said "I can accept that Jesus was a god, but I don't think he was a human being." The reason was, she explained, that a human being could not do the miracles that Jesus performed. Such sentiments are not new. There are signs that John wrote to a context where some questioned the humanity of Jesus. John emphasised how he had seen and touched Jesus (1 John 1:1). Confessing that Jesus "has come in the flesh" was a sign of orthodoxy (1 John 4:2). In the life of Jesus we see evidence of his true humanity. We see him, for example, eating and sleeping. It was essential that Jesus be truly human for him to save us and to represent us before God (1 Timothy 2:5; Hebrews 2:14–15). Nevertheless, the trinitarian question is this: Is Jesus truly God?

## The divinity of Jesus

We are going to pile up the New Testament evidence for the divinity of Christ and some readers may want to skim through what follows. But the identity of Christ is so central to the doctrine of the Trinity, and indeed to the Christian gospel, that the issues cannot be ignored.

### The acts of Jesus

What caused good monotheistic Jews to worship Jesus as God? We should not think for a moment that this was a straightforward move. Imagine you were one of Jesus' first disciples. You would not just have 20, 30 or 40 years of monotheistic thinking behind you, you would have inherited *centuries* of faith in one God running back to the Shema and beyond. Monotheism ran deep in Old Testament religion. Anything else was idolatry. To worship an image of God was forbidden. To worship a human being was unthinkable.

John begins his first letter by saying that he proclaims "that which was from the beginning...which was with the Father...his Son, Jesus Christ". This declaration of a divine Son was rooted in "that...which we have heard, which we have seen with our eyes, which we have looked at and our hands have touched" (1 John 1:1–3). The disciples confessed Jesus as God because they had known him, seen him and heard him. They encountered a man and, as they saw the things he did, they were forced to recognise that he was God in human form. Not only that, but this man was raised from the dead never to die again. Jesus Christ our Lord, says Paul, "was declared to be the Son of God in power according to the Spirit of holiness by his resurrection from the dead" (Romans 1:4, ESV).

Consider the following incident:

Immediately Jesus made the disciples get into the boat and go on ahead of him to the other side, while he dismissed the crowd. After he had dismissed them, he went up on a mountainside by himself to pray. When evening came, he was there alone, but the boat was already a considerable distance from land, buffeted by the waves because the wind was against it.

During the fourth watch of the night Jesus went out to them, walking on the lake. When the disciples saw him walking on the lake, they were terrified. "It's a ghost," they said, and cried out in fear.

But Jesus immediately said to them: "Take courage! It is I. Don't be afraid."

"Lord, if it's you," Peter replied, "tell me to come to you on the water."

"Come," he said.

Then Peter got down out of the boat, walked on the water and came towards Jesus. But when he saw the wind, he was afraid and, beginning to sink, cried out, "Lord, save me!"

> Immediately Jesus reached out his hand and caught him. "You of little faith," he said, "why did you doubt?"
> And when they climbed into the boat, the wind died down. Then those who were in the boat worshipped him, saying, "Truly you are the Son of God." (Matthew 14:22–33)

There are several indicators of the true identity of Jesus in this story.

1. The first and most obvious is the unparalleled display of power we see here. Jesus first walks on water and then stills a storm. Many people have been able to heal others – perhaps by encouraging psychosomatic responses, perhaps through the agency of a spirit. Many have done so through the power of God. But the miracles of Jesus are unique. At the very least we must say that this person is the agent of God with the power of God.

2. Jesus calls out: "Take courage! It is I." The words "it is I" are used in the Greek version of the Old Testament to translate Yahweh's self-designation as I AM in Exodus 3:14 and its echoes in Isaiah (Isaiah 41:4; 43:10, 25; 46:4; 51:12; 52:6). Particularly striking is its use in Isaiah 43:10 where it is linked to the uniqueness of God. "'You are my witnesses,' declares the LORD, 'and my servant whom I have chosen, so that you may know and believe me and understand that *I am he*. Before me no god was formed, nor will there be one after me'" (Isaiah 43:10, my emphasis). There will be no gods after Yahweh. Whatever it means for Jesus to be divine, it cannot mean he is a new God. He must be Yahweh or no God at all.

3. In Psalm 89:9 we read of God: "You rule over the surging sea; when its waves mount up, you still them." God has authority over the natural world because he is its Creator (Psalm 89:11). So to still the

sea is an act of the Creator God. Yet this is precisely the act that has now been performed by Jesus of Nazareth. Again, the quote from the Psalm is set in the context of an affirmation of monotheism (Psalm 89:6–8). No one can compare with Yahweh and no one can match his power. But now here is one who does compare and who can match his power.

4. These references to the Old Testament might appear to be a case of theologising after the event. But the implications of what Jesus has done are immediately apparent to the disciples who witnessed it. "Then those who were in the boat worshipped him, saying, 'Truly you are the Son of God'" (Matthew 14:33). They confess Jesus is the Son of God and they worship him – something that no monotheistic Jew would do except to God himself.

### The words of Jesus

In proclaiming Jesus as the divine Son of the Father, John points not only to what he has seen, but also to what he has heard (1 John 1:1–3). The words of Jesus testify to his divinity. Consider the following words of Jesus:

> Jesus gave them this answer: "I tell you the truth, the Son can do nothing by himself; he can do only what he sees his Father doing, because whatever the Father does the Son also does. For the Father loves the Son and shows him all he does. Yes, to your amazement he will show him even greater things than these. For just as the Father raises the dead and gives them life, even so the Son gives life to whom he is pleased to give it. Moreover, the Father judges no one, but has entrusted all judgment to the Son, that all may honour the Son just as they honour the Father. He who does not honour the Son does not honour the Father, who sent him. I tell you the truth, whoever hears my word and believes him who sent me has eternal life and will not be condemned; he has crossed over from death to life." (John 5:19–24)

Notice:

- the identity of the will of the Father and the Son;
- the intimate love of the Father for the Son (see also John 10:17; 14:31; 17:23);
- the Son has equal authority with the Father to give life and to judge (see also John 5:26–29; 6:40; 8:16);
- the Father and Son are equally to be honoured;
- to dishonour the Son is to dishonour the Father.

In John's Gospel Jesus clearly echoes the I AM by which Yahweh designates himself in Exodus 3:14 (John 6:20, 35, 48; 8:12, 24, 28; 9:5; 10:9, 11, 14; 11:25; 13:19; 14:6; 15:1, 5; 18:5). In John 8:58 Jesus says to the Jewish leaders: "I tell you the truth...before Abraham was born, I am!" He is claiming both to be Yahweh and to pre-exist his human birth. The Jews understand the full import of this statement for they immediately try to stone him for blasphemy (John 8:59).

### The testimony of the Apostles

John begins his Gospel: "In the beginning was the Word, and the Word was with God, and the Word was God. He was with God in the beginning. Through him all things were made; without him nothing was made that has been made" (John 1:1–3). John identifies Jesus with the Word of God. A lot of attention has focused on the idea of "word" or "reason" (*logos*) in Greek philosophy, but the Word of God is also firmly rooted in the Old Testament. God creates and rules by his Word (Psalm 33:6–9; Isaiah 55:10–11) and his Word is often personified (Psalm 107:20; 119:89; 147:15; see also Wisdom 18:15–16). John portrays Jesus, the Word of God, as divine. He is "in the beginning". He is the agent by which God creates all things. And notice how the Word is both differentiated from God ("the Word was with God") and identified with God ("the Word was God"). John goes on to describe the Word as the life and the light, and how the Word became flesh and dwelt among us. In verse 17 he brings his prologue to a climax as he identifies the Word as Jesus. And then he describes Jesus as "the only God" who uniquely makes the Father known (John 1:18, ESV). He echoes the Old Testament claim that no one has seen God, but now in the person of Jesus God can be seen and known (see also John 14:6–11).

In the Epistles Jesus is also described as God:

> Theirs are the patriarchs, and from them is traced the human ancestry of Christ, who is God over all, for ever praised! Amen. (Romans 9:5)

> In Christ all the fulness of the Deity lives in bodily form. (Colossians 2:9)

> ... while we wait for the blessed hope – the glorious appearing of our great God and Saviour, Jesus Christ. (Titus 2:13)

> But about the Son he says, "Your throne, O God, will last for ever and ever, and righteousness will be the sceptre of your kingdom." (Hebrews 1:8)

> To those who through the righteousness of our God and Saviour Jesus Christ have received a faith as precious as ours. (2 Peter 1:1)

> We are in him who is true – even in his Son Jesus Christ. He is the true God and eternal life. (1 John 5:20)

Titus 2:13 and 2 Peter 1:1 could refer to God and Saviour as distinct entities, but the most natural reading is that which sees them as a double description of one person.

## Jesus as the Son of God

In the Old Testament Israel is described as the son of God (Exodus 4:22–23; Hosea 11:1). In time the Israelite king was called the son of God (2 Samuel 7:14; Psalm 2:7). In the New Testament the description of Jesus as God's Son often has this background in mind. It is not necessarily an affirmation of deity, but of Jesus as the true Israel and the promised Davidic king (see Mark 1:11; Acts 13:32–33). But in John's Gospel the sonship of Jesus finds its fullest expression: "And the Word became flesh and dwelt among us, and we have seen his glory, glory as of the only Son from the Father, full of grace and truth" (John 1:14, ESV). Here the sonship of Jesus refers to his unique relationship to the Father as the pre-existent Word of God. Two verses previously John talks about believers being "children of God" (John 1:12), but here he consciously distinguishes Jesus as "the only Son from the Father". Jesus is not just a human person who fulfils Old Testament hopes, nor the paradigm of a faithful believer. He is the One sent from the Father by the Father: "I came from the Father and entered the world; now I am leaving the world and going back to the Father" (John 16:28). Paul, too, speaks of Jesus as "the Son of God" (Romans 1:4; Galatians 2:20; Ephesians 4:13) and "the Son" (Romans 1:2, 9; 5:10; 8:3, 29, 32; 1 Corinthians 1:9; 15:28; Galatians 1:16; 4:4, 6; Colossians 1:13; 1 Thessalonians 1:10). Paul uses the definite article – *the* Son – indicating the uniquely divine sonship of Jesus. In Romans 8 Paul describes how we have become the sons of God (8:13–17). But this is only possible because God sent "his *own* Son" (8:3, 32, my emphasis).

The writer to Hebrews begins his letter with these words:

> In the past God spoke to our forefathers through the prophets at many times and in various ways, but in these last days he has spo-

ken to us by his Son, whom he appointed heir of all things, and through whom he made the universe. The Son is the radiance of God's glory and the exact representation of his being, sustaining all things by his powerful word. After he had provided purification for sins, he sat down at the right hand of the Majesty in heaven. So he became as much superior to the angels as the name he has inherited is superior to theirs. (Hebrews 1:1–4)

Notice:

- Jesus is described as the Son and heir of God;
- Jesus is said to be the agent of creation and the one who sustains the universe;
- Jesus is "the radiance of God's glory and the exact representation of his being";
- he shares a position of honour with "the Majesty in heaven";
- he is more than an exulted creature for he is superior to the most exalted creatures.

Jesus so perfectly reveals God that he is "the exact imprint of his nature" Hebrews 1:3, ESV). His revelation is identical to that which is revealed to such a perfect degree that he *is* God. Imagine a poet writing a poem. Inevitably the poet expresses something of themselves in the poem. The poem gives us a window onto their thoughts and emotions. Now imagine God as an infinite and perfect poet who speaks a Word which so fully expresses himself that it is one with himself. Jesus is that eternal Word, revealing the Father and identical to the Father in every way except that the Son is the revelation while the Father is the one who reveals.

With the designation of Jesus as the divine Son, so the first person of the Trinity is designated as the Father. God is not simply like a father. The first person of the Trinity is the "Father of our Lord Jesus Christ" (Romans 15:5–6;

2 Corinthians 1:3; 11:31; Ephesians 1:3; Colossians 1:3; 1 Peter 1:3). Before God is our Father, he is the Father of Jesus Christ. We know God as Father only through our union with the divine Son.

## Jesus as Yahweh

One of the earliest Christian creeds was the confession that "Jesus is Lord" (Romans 10:9; 1 Corinthians 12:1–3; Philippians 2:9–11). In the first century AD the word "Lord" was often used of masters and distinguished people. In the hierarchy of Roman society the supreme Lord was the Emperor. To confess Jesus as Lord was to claim that he was your ultimate authority. It was a confession of an allegiance that superseded other allegiances – even allegiance to Caesar.

But the word "Lord" was not just a Roman term. It was also a Jewish term. It is the word use to translate "Yahweh" in the Greek version of the Old Testament. When the first Christians confessed Jesus as Lord they were not only acknowledging him to be the true Emperor. They were saying that he was Yahweh, the God of Israel. Christians are described as those who "call on the name of the Lord" where the Lord is clearly Jesus (1 Corinthians 1:2; see also Acts 9:13–14; 22:16). But this is also a clear echo of Old Testament passages that speak of calling on the name of Yahweh (Psalm 99:6; 105:1; Joel 2:32).

When Jesus calls himself "the good shepherd" he is alluding to passages in the Old Testament that speak of Yahweh's role as the shepherd of his people (John 10:11; Psalm 23:1; Ezekiel 34:11–16). Likewise, Jesus is described as a bridegroom with his people as the bride (2 Corinthians 11:2; Ephesians 5:25) – a reference to the relationship of Yahweh to his people (Isaiah 54:5; Hosea 2:20). What is interesting is that Jesus takes the place of God's people in other Old Testament images. He is "the true vine" in contrast to faithless Israel (John 15:1; Isaiah 5:1–7). Jesus is both Yahweh and Yahweh's people. He is the God-man who represents both God and humanity and so is able to mediate between the two (1 Timothy 2:5).

Yet while we can say Jesus is Yahweh, we cannot say Yahweh is Jesus. Jesus is also differentiated from God. Throughout his ministry Jesus prays to God. He commends his spirit to God as he dies. Jesus is identified as God, but Jesus is not identical to God.

## *Jesus as an object of worship*

Arthur Wainwright claims that "probably [Jesus] was recognised as God in worship earlier than in reflective thought," though he concedes we cannot know this for sure.[6] Certainly some of the earliest Christian hymns contain strong expressions of the divinity of Christ. Although Colossians 1:15–20 and Philippians 2:6–11, for example, are not explicitly addressed to Jesus as the object of worship, both involve strong affirmations of Christ's divinity. In other passages worship is addressed to Christ:

> The Lord will rescue me from every evil attack and will bring me safely to his heavenly kingdom. To him be glory for ever and ever. Amen. (2 Timothy 4:18)

> May the God of peace, who through the blood of the eternal covenant brought back from the dead our Lord Jesus, that great Shepherd of the sheep, equip you with everything good for doing his will, and may he work in us what is pleasing to him, through Jesus Christ, to whom be glory for ever and ever. Amen. (Hebrews 13:20–21)

> But grow in the grace and knowledge of our Lord and Saviour Jesus Christ. To him be glory both now and for ever! Amen. (2 Peter 3:18)

---

6. Arthur W. Wainwright, *The Trinity in the New Testament* (SPCK, 1962), p. 10.

> You are worthy to take the scroll and to open its seals, because you were slain, and with your blood you purchased men for God from every tribe and language and people and nation. You have made them to be a kingdom and priests to serve our God, and they will reign on the earth. (Revelation 5:9–10; see also Revelation 7:10)

We have already seen how during his life Jesus was worshipped (Matthew 14:33). After his resurrection Thomas confesses before Jesus: "My Lord and my God!" (John 20:28). As Stephen is stoned to death he calls out "Lord Jesus, receive my spirit" (Acts 7:59). And Paul addresses prayer to Jesus or to the Father and Jesus (1 Corinthians 16:22; 2 Corinthians 12:8; 1 Thessalonians 3:11–12; Romans 1:7; 1 Corinthians 1:3).

## The Spirit of God

The Holy Spirit is spoken of as "the breath", "the presence" and "the power" of God. The Spirit is identified with both the Father and the Son. He is the Spirit of God (Romans 8:9, 11; 2 Corinthians 3:3; 1 John 4:2) and the Spirit of Jesus (Acts 16:7; Romans 8:9; Galatians 4:6; Philippians 1:19; see also 2 Corinthians 3:17–18). To lie to the Spirit is to lie to God (Acts 5:3–4). Jesus is present with the disciples through the Spirit (John 14:18, 23). The Spirit is, as it were, self-effacing. His work is "to the Father" and "to the Son". We pray through the Spirit to the Father (Romans 8:15; Ephesians 2:18). He mediates the presence of Christ among his people (John 14:16–18). He brings glory to the Son (John 16:14).

The key trinitarian question regarding the Spirit is not whether he is God, but whether he is a distinct person. Is the Spirit more than an expression of God-in-action or God-among-us? The New Testament answer is that the Spirit has a distinct identity (Mark 1:12; 13:11; Luke 4:1–2). As Jesus is baptised and as the Father speaks from heaven, the Spirit descends on Jesus in the form of a dove (Matthew 3:16–17; Mark 1:9–11; Luke 3:21–22). The Spirit listens to the Father just as Jesus did (John 16:13). He forbids the Apostles to preach in Asia (Acts 16:6) and warns Paul of the sufferings that await him (Acts 20:23). The Spirit has a "mind" (Romans 8:27) and Christians are to be led by the Spirit (Romans 8:14; Galatians 5:18). The Spirit is also differentiated from the Father and the Son. He is sent by the Father (John 14:16, 26; Galatians 4:6) and he is sent by Jesus (John 15:26). When Jesus returns to the Father, the Spirit will replace him (John 16:7).

In Greek the word "Spirit" is neuter. It should be referred to as "it", but most of the time the New Testament talks about the Holy Spirit as "he" and uses personal pronouns of the Spirit (John 14:26; 15:26; 16:8, 14). Jesus talks of him as the Paraclete – a Greek word not easily translated that combines the ideas of "advocate" and "comforter" (John 14:16, 26). The personhood of the Spirit is implied in what is said of him. Paul warns against "grieving" the Holy Spirit (Ephesians 4:30). People can speak or blaspheme against the Holy Spirit (Matthew 12:32; Mark 3:28–29). The Spirit, as we have seen, acts as a distinct agent.

## Towards a doctrine of the Trinity

It would be wrong to say that the New Testament contains a doctrine of the Trinity in the way that we now conceive it. The concerns of the New Testament writers were elsewhere. But there are, nevertheless, signs of a trinitarian awareness. The early church had to find new ways of describing what they had experienced. We see emerging triadic statements. Paul, for example, offers a prayer which has become common in all churches: "May the grace of the Lord Jesus Christ, and the love of God, and the fellowship of the Holy Spirit be with you all" (2 Corinthians 13:14). As Ben Witherington and Laura Ice comment, "Paul is at least functionally trinitarian."[7] We find other statements concerning Father, Son and Spirit in Romans 14:17–18; 15:16, 30; 1 Corinthians 12:4–6; 2 Corinthians 1:21–22; 3:3; Galatians 4:4–6; Ephesians 2:18; 3:14–17; Colossians 1:3–8; 2 Thessalonians 2:13–14 and Titus 3:4–7. These triadic statements have a basis in Christ's own commission of his disciples to "go and make disciples of all nations, baptising them in the name of the Father and of the Son and of the Holy Spirit" (Matthew 28:19). This baptismal formula is significant. Paul links one baptism with one God (Ephesians 4:4–6), but this one God is described as three persons in baptism. Indeed not only are there signs of a trinitarian awareness, but also of an emerging sense of trinitarian orthodoxy. John says: "No one who denies the Son has the Father; whoever acknowledges the Son has the Father also" (1 John 2:23).

I once wrote an essay on how the fact that Christians are united to Christ should affect the way we live. At the top of my paper my tutor wrote "Calvin". Apparently my view was similar to that of John Calvin, the great six-teenth-century Reformer. I had never read anything by Calvin, but I had been brought up in circles in which he was revered. Indirectly, it seemed, I had imbibed some-thing of his thinking. When I started reading Calvin, my understanding of our union with Christ grew and deep-ened. I acquired a vocabulary that helped me grasp and talk about it (words like "mortification" and "vivifica-tion"). It was probably something like that with the doc-trine of the Trinity. People like Paul were trinitarian even though they did not have the vocabulary, because they

---

7. Ben Witherington III and Laura Ice, *The Shadow of the Almighty: Father, Son and Spirit in Biblical Perspective* (Eerdmans, 2002), p. 135.

lived and thought in the context of God's trinitarian actions towards the world. The vocabulary would come later, helping help us understand and talk about the Trinity. But all the ingredients of trinitarianism are there in the New Testament. We can summarise the biblical data as follows:

- there is one God;
- the Father, the Son and the Spirit are God;
- the Father, the Son and the Spirit are differentiated in that the Father is not the Son or the Spirit, nor is the Son the Spirit.

How later generations of Christians put these truths together is the subject of Part Two. But before that, in Chapter 4, we will explore how the trinitarian nature of God is revealed supremely in the cross.

In this chapter we have seen that Jesus and the Spirit are God. They are not simply godlike. They are not simply God's representatives. They are God himself. "In Christ," says Paul, "all the fulness of the Deity lives in bodily form" (Colossians 2:9–10). Jesus does more than show us something about God. He is God.

I remember walking to meet a friend of mine. He had just heard that the woman he hoped to marry had been killed in a car accident. What was I going to say? I had no idea. I did not want to spin out empty platitudes. But I did want to speak a word of gospel comfort. As it turned out my task was easy. I simply listened as he spoke those words of gospel comfort to himself – and me. Of course he spoke of the deep pain in his heart; his reddened eyes were testimony to that. But he spoke, too, of the love of Jesus. He could not understand why God had allowed his loved one to die, but he knew that God was not immune to his suffering. Jesus knew what it was like to be human.

He knew what it was like to suffer the effects of sin. He knew what it was like to lose a friend. He had wept. And this Jesus was God. God knew what it was to be human, to suffer, to lose a friend. In those dark moments after his loss, my friend found comfort in a God who had entered our world and shared our experience.

# Chapter 4

# Unity and plurality
# at the cross

Mark 15:39 must surely be one of the most remarkable statements in the Bible: "When the centurion, who stood there in front of Jesus, heard his cry and saw how he died, he said, 'Surely this man was the Son of God!'" (Mark 15:39). What has the centurion seen? He has seen a criminal executed. What last words has he heard? "My God, my God, why have you forsaken me?" (Mark 15:34). Yet he says: "Surely this man was the Son of God!"

Moreover, this is not a throwaway comment. It is the climax of Mark's Gospel. We do not know what led the centurion to make the statement. But we can know what Mark was thinking. He begins his Gospel: "The beginning of the gospel about Jesus Christ, the Son of God" (Mark 1:1). He makes two statements about Jesus that set the agenda for his account of Jesus' life. Jesus is the "Christ" and "the Son of God". The first half of the Gospel comes to a climax with Peter's confession that Jesus is the Christ (Mark 8:29). Jesus then begins to teach his disciples what kind of a Christ he is – he is the Christ who must suffer and die. This is the theme of the second half of the Gospel. The disciples struggle to accept this, let alone make it the model for their lives. They want power without service and glory without shame. The centurion's confession is the climax of the second half of the Gospel. He confesses that Jesus is the Son of God, but he does so as he sees Jesus die. Jesus is the Christ and the Son of God, and the cross is the ultimate revelation of his identity.

At the moment at which God is most absent, the centurion sees the presence of the living God. It is extraordinary. This godforsaken moment is the very point at which the centurion recognises God. God is revealed by the absence of God. Martin Luther contrasted theologians of glory with theologians of the cross. Theologians of glory look for God in creation, miraculous signs, spiritual experience or human wisdom. If such knowledge were available, argued Luther, it would lead to pride. God is known only through revelation, but this revelation is hidden so that it shatters human pretensions. God is revealed in what is contrary. The wisdom of God is hidden in the folly of the cross. The glory of God is hidden in the shame of the cross. The power of God is hidden in the weakness of the cross. So if we want to discover the true character of God we must look to the cross. And the God revealed in the cross is trinitarian. He is both single and plural; one united being and three distinct persons.

## God forsaken by God

In his account of the final days of Jesus' life, Mark describes how Jesus is forsaken by humanity. He is betrayed by a kiss, deserted by his friends, disowned by Peter. He is judged, tortured and killed by humanity. But now Mark reveals an even greater mystery: "And at the ninth hour Jesus cried out in a loud voice, '*Eloi, Eloi, lema sabachthani*?' which means, 'My God, my God, why have you forsaken me?'" (Mark 15:34). We will never grasp the full import of these words. The abandonment of Jesus by humanity is eclipsed by his abandonment by God. At his baptism the heavens were "torn open" (Mark 1:10), but now heaven is closed. Jesus is forsaken by God. The Son is abandoned by his Father to death.

In the moment of the Son's greatest need and greatest pain, God is not there. The Son cries and is not heard. The familiar resource, the ultimate resource, the only resource, is not there. The God who was always there, the God who was needed now as He had never been needed before, was nowhere to be seen. There was no answer to the Son's cry. There was no comfort. Jesus was left God-less, with no perception of His own Sonship, unable for the one and only time in His life to say, "Abba, Father." He was left with no sense of God's love and no sense of the operation of God's purpose. There was nothing but that *"Why?"*, trying vainly to bridge the Darkness. He was sin. He was lawlessness, and as such He was banished to the Black Hole where lawlessness belongs and from which no sound can escape but, *"Why?"* That was the Son's only word in His final agony as He reached out to God whom He needed so desperately but whom as Sin He couldn't discern and from whose presence He was outcast. There could be no accord. "God His Son not Sparing"! He had to be dealt with not as Son but as Sin.[1]

The Father and the Son love one another with a perfect love throughout eternity. To see Jesus is to know the Father. But now they are torn apart. The divine community is broken. The Father and the Son who mutually indwell one another are separated. The Father experiences the loss of his Son. The Son endures the judicial abandonment of his Father. Jesus dies bearing the full effects of sin and the full force of God's wrath. He is alone and abandoned. The distinction of the divine persons is expressed in the most extreme way: God is divided from God.

That God should be divided from God only makes sense if God is a trinitarian community. Only if there is some distinction within God could it ever be possible for God to be forsaken by God.

---

1.  Donald Macleod, *A Faith to Live By* (Mentor, 1998), pp. 130–131.

## God uniting to God

The cross reveals not only the distinctions within God, but also the common purpose of the godhead: to reconcile humanity to himself. As Jesus breathed his last we read: "The curtain of the temple was torn in two from top to bottom" (Mark 15:38). The temple was the symbol of God's presence with his people (see Hebrews 9). But its physical structure taught that God was unapproachable. It involved a series of courts which only certain people were allowed to progress through. The innermost place was the Holiest of Holies, which was separated from the people by a curtain as thick as a person's hand. Imagine a heist movie with a gang of thieves trying to break into a bank. A whole series of security measures keep them from the vault, but the final obstacle is an impenetrable steel door with a complex locking mechanism. Such was the curtain of the temple. Only the High Priest was allowed to enter, and only once a year, and only through the shedding of blood. It was a graphic reminder that sinful people are cut off from God.

But as Jesus died the curtain separating God from humanity was torn in two. The way to God had been opened. He is now knowable and approachable. Separated from God, Jesus united us to God. The trinitarian community is a welcoming community. We are invited to share its life and enjoy its love. Jesus has died in our place so that we can be family. Even as the Father and Son were separated by the Father's judicial abandonment, they were united in a common purpose to save God's people.

If we distance *the persons* of the Trinity from one another then we distance *the work* of the divine persons. It is a short step then mistakenly to see either the Father or the Son as an unwilling participant in the events of Calvary.

## Mistake #1: An unwilling Father placated by the Son

If we do not maintain the unity of the Trinity then the Father can become a severe, authority figure who is placated by the loving Son. We may even think the Father is unwilling to forgive without the intervention of the Son. We imagine a fearful, distant Father and create as his counterpart a loving Son. But just as the Son experienced abandonment by the Father, so the Father experienced the loss of his Son. He gave him up. Jürgen Moltmann says: "The Son suffers in his love being forsaken by the Father as he dies. The Father suffers in his love the grief of the death of the Son."[2] Our salvation is not wrestled reluctantly from the Father. It begins in his eternal love (Ephesians 1:3–4). "For God so loved the world that he gave his... only Son..." (John 3:16). And it is achieved at the expense of that which he loved most – his own Son. Donald Macleod says: "We are at the outer parameters of revelation here, but we have to accept the New Testament's constant emphasis that the cost of our redemption was borne not only by God the Son but by God the Father."[3]

## Mistake #2: An unwilling Son victimised by the Father

Alternatively, if we separate the persons and work of the Trinity, we may view the Son as the unwilling victim of the Father's justice. The night before he died, Jesus prayed in Gethsemane: "Abba, Father, all things are possible for you. Remove this cup from me. Yet not what I will, but what you will" (Mark 14:36, ESV). We should not view this as an unwilling submission to a will which is alien to him. When the daughter of friends of ours was three years old she fell into an icy river. Fortunately her arms caught on the ice so that she was not fully submerged.

---

2. Jürgen Moltmann, *The Crucified God* (SCM, 1974), p. 245.
3. Donald Macleod, *A Faith to Live By*, p. 131.

Immediately her father jumped in and pulled her out. If you had frozen time before he jumped and asked him whether he wanted to jump in he would have answered "Yes" and "No". At one level, he did not want to enter the icy waters – there was no pleasure in it! Yet at another level the answer was clearly "Yes" – his paternal love overcame any regard for personal discomfort so he jumped willingly. The same is true of Jesus. As he looked ahead in Gethsemane to his separation from God, he recoiled from it. If there had been another way he would have taken it. But he went to the cross willingly. He went willingly because of his love for his people.

Neither portrayal of the Father or of the Son as unwilling participants in the cross is true to the biblical account which affirms the unity of Father and Son in salvation. The Son does the will of the Father. Their wills are one and the same. Paul says: "God was reconciling the world to himself in Christ" (2 Corinthians 5:19). The Father and the Son were acting together to reconcile the world. "Even at the moment of deepest darkness, God the Father and God the Son were acting together to bring about a reconciliation with the world."[4] Their unity at the cross is more than a unity of wills. It remains a unity of being. The God of the cross is the God of the Shema – one, single, undivided (Deuteronomy 6:4). The experience of the cross does not happen to another. God is not forsaking another. He is not judging another. God is forsaking himself. He is judging himself.

> The judge and the victim are not two different beings. Jesus and the Father are one (John 10:30), just as the Lord is the Spirit (2 Corinthians 3:17). On Calvary, Jehovah condemns sin. He curses it. He puts it outside (Hebrews 13:12). Equally, however, He bears it. He imputes it to Himself. He receives its wages. He becomes Himself

---

4. Michael Jenson, "The Very Practical Doctrine of the Trinity", *The Briefing* 249 (March 2001), p. 14.

its propitiation. He becomes the sinner's ransom. He becomes even the sinner's advocate – God with God. Certainly, we must not ignore or obscure the distinction between God the Father and God the Son. Equally, however, we must avoid the more prevalent danger of regarding the Father and the Son as different beings. In the last analysis, God expresses His love for us not by putting another to suffer in our place, but by Himself taking our place. He meets the whole cost of our forgiveness in Himself by exacting it of Himself. He demands the ransom, He provides the ransom. He becomes the ransom. Herein is love.[5]

In 1794 William Carey, the great missionary to India, found the remains of a child being eaten by white ants. The child had been offered as a sacrifice to the gods. A sick infant was thought to be under the power of an evil spirit. To purge the family of its influence, the child was hung in a basket for three days. Only if the child was still alive after the three days would attempts be made to save it. On the winter solstice at Sagar Island, where the River Ganges meets the sea, children were pushed down the mud banks into the sea where they would drown or be eaten by crocodiles. This was considered a holy sacrifice which atoned for the sins of the family. Carey researched these practices, published reports and petitioned the Government. Eventually infanticide was declared illegal – the first time the British Government had directly interfered in the religious practices of India. In 1804 Carey visited Sagar Island. As Carey stood on the banks of the river he proclaimed the story of God's own sacrifice. God has sacrificed his Son for our sins so that we need never sacrifice our children. We cannot, nor do we need to, appease the gods. The triune God has himself made atonement.[6]

---

5. Donald Macleod, *Behold Your God* (Christian Focus, 1990, 2nd ed., 1995), p. 184.
6. See Ruth and Vishal Mangalwadi, *Carey, Christ and Cultural Transformation: The Life and Influence of William Carey* (OM, 1993), pp. 14–15.

## God revealing God

The cross is not only an act of redemption. It is also an act of revelation. The confession of the centurion draws our attention to this (Mark 15:39). The cross is not God acting out of character. It is God revealing his character.

### The divinity of Jesus on trial

Why was Jesus killed? The answer to this question is not straightforward. Clearly Jesus died because this was the will of God. His death was the means by which God reconciles us to himself. But why was Jesus killed by the human authorities? What was his crime? The answer is multifaceted. His message of divine grace subverted the status of the religious elite. His message of God's coming reign subverted the political power of empire. But in his account of the trial of Jesus, Mark presents the issue as one of blasphemy. Jesus is killed because he claimed to be God.

> The high priest asked him, "Are you the Christ, the Son of the Blessed One?" "I am," said Jesus. "And you will see the Son of Man sitting at the right hand of the Mighty One and coming on the clouds of heaven." The high priest tore his clothes. "Why do we need any more witnesses?" he asked. "You have heard the blasphemy. What do you think?" They all condemned him as worthy of death. (Mark 14:61–64)

"The Son of the Blessed One" is a case of Jewish circumlocution. To avoid directly using the name of God, the Jews used other words like "Blessed One". Jesus replies with another circumlocution, describing God as "the Mighty One". So when the High Priest asked if Jesus was "the Son of the Blessed One" he was asking Jesus whether he was the divine Son. Jesus answers: "I am". The words "I am" allude to God's description of himself to Moses as I AM in Exodus 3:14. Jesus then combines two references from Psalm 110:1 and Daniel 7:13–14. Both passages describe the conflict between God's people and the world, and promise the vindication of God's people. In using them Jesus is claiming that this ongoing conflict is now focused on his trial and his claim to divinity. And he is claiming that the outcome of his trial will not be the last word. Jesus will be vindicated by God. The meaning of Jesus' words is clear enough to the Jewish leaders. The High Priest tears his garments and the assembly condemns Jesus as a blasphemer. They recognise that Jesus is claiming to be God, but they judge this a false claim. Humanity has condemned Jesus as a blasphemer, but Jesus claims his divinity will be vindicated by God. At the cross the ultimate verdict hangs in the balance. But as far as Mark is concerned the centurion makes the true judgment when he declares that Jesus is the Son of God – a judgment that anticipates the vindication of Jesus by God.

### The Spirit's verdict: Presence

In Hebrew 9:14 we find a somewhat enigmatic reference to the Spirit: "How much more … will the blood of *Christ, who through the eternal Spirit offered himself unblemished to God*, cleanse our consciences from acts that lead to death, so that we may serve the living God!" (my emphasis). At his baptism the Spirit came upon Christ, empowering him for ministry. The writer of Hebrews suggests that this divine empowerment continues to the climax of Jesus' ministry as he offers himself for his people. On the cross Jesus is abandoned by his Father, but the Spirit is present with him enabling him to offer himself to the Father. "This text shows how the obedience and love of Christ for the Father reached its perfection in his voluntary self-offering on the cross, and that this act, which gathered up and re-expressed the obedience and love that characterised his whole life, was performed in the power of the Holy Spirit conferred on him by God."[7] Even in death Christ is sovereign. He is not the victim of the Roman authorities, still less is he the passive victim of his Father. Through the Spirit he is the agent of his own death, freely offering himself in love for his people (John 10:18). Calvin comments: "Christ suffered as man, but in order that His death might effect our salvation it came forth from the power of the Spirit. The sacrifice of eternal atonement was a more than human work."[8]

The prayer of Gethsemane, "Abba, Father" (Mark 14:36), is picked up in Romans 8:15 and Galatians 4:6. These are the only other direct references to God as "Abba" in the New Testament. In Romans and Galatians it is a prayer offered by Christians *through the Spirit*. The Spirit's role is emphasised. It suggests that Jesus, too, offered the prayer of Gethsemane through the Spirit. As the disciples slept because their flesh was weak, Jesus prayed because he was sustained by the Spirit. Through the Spirit he submitted to the Father's will. Just as the Spirit enables Christians to follow the way of the cross, so the Spirit enabled Jesus freely to choose the cross. His passion from Gethsemane to his final breath was conducted through the Spirit. Jürgen Moltmann says:

> Mark is giving a pneumatological interpretation of Jesus' passion – the passion which begins in Gethsemane with the experience of God's hiddenness, and ends with the experience of God-forsakenness on the cross. What begins with his baptism through the operation of the Spirit ends in his passion through the operation of the Spirit. The Spirit which "leads" Jesus into the wilderness is beside him, sustaining him in his suffering from God.[9]

7. David Coffey, Deus Trinitas: *The Doctrine of the Triune God* (OUP, 1999), p. 40.
8. John Calvin, *Hebrews and First and Second Peter* (St Andrews Press, 1963), p. 121.
9. Jürgen Moltmann, *The Spirit of Life: A Universal Affirmation* (SCM, 1992), pp. 63–64.

### The Spirit's verdict: Resurrection

The death of Jesus is not the final word. As we have seen, in Mark 14 Jesus quotes Psalm 110 and Daniel 7 to claim that he will be vindicated in the face of those who deny his divinity. And so it was. In Romans 1:4 we read that Jesus "through the Spirit of holiness was declared with power to be the Son of God, by his resurrection from the dead". The Spirit vindicates the divinity of Jesus by raising him from the dead (1 Timothy 3:16). The verdict of the trial – the verdict of the world – is that Jesus is a blasphemer. But God through his Spirit overturns that verdict in the court of appeal.

### The Spirit's verdict: Revelation

To see the presence of God in the absence of God; to see the revelation of God in the death of a man – this is an act of faith. And such faith can only be a work of God within us. Writing to the Corinthians, Paul says:

> I resolved to know nothing while I was with you except Jesus Christ and him crucified… My message and my preaching were not with wise and persuasive words, but with a demonstration of the Spirit's power, so that your faith might not rest on men's wisdom, but on God's power. (1 Corinthians 2:2–5)

Acceptance of the message of Christ crucified is a work of the Spirit. The god of the philosophers – typified for Paul in the Greeks – is known through wisdom. The god of religious people – typified for Paul in his fellow Jews – is known through miraculous signs (1 Corinthians 1:22). But Paul himself refuses to preach anything but "Christ crucified" (1 Corinthians 1:23). God is revealed not through wisdom, nor through miracles, but in the hiddenness of the cross. Only faith perceives, in the folly of the cross, the true wisdom of God. Only faith perceives, in the weakness of the cross, the true power of God. And such faith is the work of the divine Spirit. As the cross is preached people confess Jesus as Lord through the Spirit. This is the way by which Jesus is vindicated and glorified.

## Conclusion

### We need the cross to make sense of the Trinity
Creation may point to God's "eternal power and divine nature" (Romans 1:20), but it does not reveal his trinitarian identity. All analogies drawn from nature fall short of explaining the mystery of the Trinity. But neither does Scripture explicitly reveal the Trinity – not in the sense of providing texts that set it out for us. Ultimately it is the cross that secures the doctrine of the Trinity. "Forsaking" is an interpersonal term. The cross makes it possible for us to understand the Trinity as a community of persons in relationship.

### We need the Trinity to make sense of the cross
We cannot understand the cross without the plurality of God. The cross shows us that there are distinctions within God. God can be forsaken by God. But neither can we understand the cross without the unity of God. If God is not one then the cross becomes a cruel and vindictive act with an angry Father punishing an unwilling Son or a loving Son placating an unwilling Father. Only if God is one can the cross be for us reconciliation and inclusion within the divine community.

We have already seen how in Philippians Chapter 2 Paul quotes from Isaiah 45:21–23, one of the classic Old Testament assertions of monotheism:

> And there is no God apart from me,
> a righteous God and a Saviour;
> there is none but me.
> Turn to me and be saved,

all you ends of the earth;
for I am God, and there is no other.
By myself I have sworn,
my mouth has uttered in all integrity
a word that will not be revoked:
Before me every knee will bow;
by me every tongue will swear. (Isaiah 45:21–23)

Paul takes this great monotheistic statement and applies it to Christ. Christ will receive the allegiance of every knee and every tongue that is due to the one God. But in Philippians Paul makes a further claim. He claims that this worship is due to Christ because "he humbled himself and became obedient to death – even death on a cross!" (Philippians 2:8). God in the person of Jesus Christ is acknowledged as God not because he has done godlike things in terms of human notions of god. It is not because he has acted in power or revealed himself in a blaze of glory. God will be acknowledged as God because he has humbled himself, and submitted to the cruel and shameful death of crucifixion. The cross alone reveals the radical, gracious freedom of God. God alone is so free that he can discount "equality with God" (Philippians 2:6) and offer himself in love for his people. God alone is so gracious that he freely chooses to be godforsaken to reconcile himself with those who have rejected him. Nothing demonstrates the godness of God so much as the godlessness of the cross.

The confession that Jesus is God not only declares something about Jesus, it also proclaims something about God. Tom Wright says: "To say that Jesus is in some sense God is of course to make a startling statement about Jesus. It is also to make a stupendous claim about God."[10] The true God is not the god of philosophy or religion. We must not assume what God is like and then ask

---

10. N. T. Wright, *Who Was Jesus?* (SPCK, 1992), p. 5.

whether Jesus fits the description. We must allow Jesus and his cross to redefine our notions of God. God is not some impersonal, ultimate Absolute. He is not a deistic god who looks on the world he has made with indifference. He is not a god who must be placated through religious duties. Nor is he a lenient god who indulgently overlooks our rebellion and the suffering it causes. He is the God of the cross. He is the God who offered himself in love to reconcile us to himself. Wright talks about how in his role as a chaplain he would talk with students about their beliefs. Many would defiantly announce to him that they did not believe in god. So he would ask them to describe the god they did not believe in. Usually they described a remote, deistic god. "I don't believe in that god either," he would reply. And then he would begin to talk about Jesus Christ.

# PART TWO
# Historical developments

# Chapter 5

# God's actions, God's being (2nd–4th centuries AD)

*The first Christian theologians thought about the Trinity as an expression of God's actions towards his creation. God had become the Trinity in history. But soon theologians began to recognise that God's actions must reflect his eternal being. Father, Son and Spirit were not different modes of God's activity, but three eternal persons sharing one divine substance.*

I have a couple of friends who are doing science PhDs. They have spent two or three years in the lab doing experiments, observing what happens, recording the facts and figures. Now they are both at the point of writing up their theses. They have a mass of data in front of them and some theories forming in their minds. Now they have to make sense of it all. They have to put it together into a coherent set of ideas. That is the point we have reached with the doctrine of the Trinity. We have made observations, especially of the life of Jesus and the impact of the Holy Spirit. The facts have been recorded in the Bible. Now we need to make sense of the data. The Bible shows us that:

- there is one God;
- the Father, the Son and the Spirit are God;
- the Father, the Son and the Spirit are differentiated in that the Father is not the Son or the Spirit, nor is the Son the Spirit.

The doctrine of the Trinity is the attempt to put this data together to create a coherent picture of God that is true to the biblical testimony and which safeguards the central truths of the gospel. A doctrine of the Trinity, in this sense, is only latent in the New Testament. It often developed in response to false ideas about the nature of Christ and the personhood of the Spirit. John Calvin summarises the biblical data with admirable brevity when he says: "Father and Son and Spirit are one God, yet the Son is not the Father, nor the Spirit the Son."[1] He says he wishes the matter could be left at that, but false understandings require us to go further. In this and the following two chapters we will look at the move from the biblical data to a doctrine of the Trinity. We will present this in the form of a story – the story of how Christians over the centuries have defended the gospel and explored the reality of the God we worship.

## The economy of God

The first Christian writers after the Apostles thought of the Trinity in terms of the "economy" of God. The Greek word for "economy" originally referred to the management of a household. The world is pictured as God's household and the economy of God is the way God "manages" the world. So when the first Christian writers talked about the Trinity they were not speculating about the eternal being of God. They were describing the way God was involved with his world in history. Irenaeus, writing in the second century AD, described the Son and the Spirit as the "two hands of God".[2] God is revealed through the story of salvation and so the earliest creeds took a narrative form. This is a baptismal liturgy from AD 215:

---

1. John Calvin, *Institutes of the Christian Religion*, 1.13.5.
2. Irenaeus, *Against Heresies*, IV.

Let the candidates stand in the water, undressed, a deacon going with them in the same way. "Do you believe in God, the Father Almighty?" "I believe." He shall baptise him once. "Do you believe in Christ Jesus, the Son of God, who was born by the Holy Spirit of the Virgin Mary, and was crucified under Pontius Pilate, and was dead and buried, and rose again on the third day, alive from the dead, and ascended into heaven, and sat at the right hand of the Father, and will come to judge the living and the dead?" "I believe." He is baptised again. "Do you believe in the Holy Spirit; in the holy church, and the resurrection of the flesh?" "I believe." He is baptised a third time.[3]

This liturgy developed into what we know as the Apostles' Creed which begins: "I believe in God, the Father Almighty, Creator of heaven and earth." Belief in God is equated with belief in the person of the Father. Monarchy (the "Almighty") and creation are attributed to the Father. In the first few centuries after Christ, the church wrestled with the question of whether the Father was over the Son and the Spirit, and maybe even their Creator. Because they focused their trinitarianism on the economy of God, the second-century writers tended to think that the threeness of God belonged to a particular period in the history of God. The Son and the Spirit came from the Father *in time* rather than eternally. The one God divided in time to become the Trinity. Justin Martyr, the second-century writer who explained Christianity to pagan audiences, described Jesus as "first-begotten" rather than eternally begotten.[4]

## Tertullian

Quintus Septimius Florens Tertullianus (c.160–c.212) was born in Carthage in what is now Tunisia. He studied law in Rome where he was converted, returning to

---

3. *Apostolic Tradition*, 21.
4. Justin, *First Apology*, 23.

Carthage to spread the gospel and defend the faith. In later years Tertullian was drawn to Montanism, an austere sect that prophesied the imminent end of the world. Tertullian was one of the first Christians to write in Latin and he is often thought of as the father of Latin, Western theology. His Latin prose was widely admired. A fifth-century writer said of him: "Almost every word he uttered was an epigram and every sentence a victory."

We get our word "Trinity" from the Latin word *trinitas*, coined by the north African theologian, Tertullian. Like other second-century Christians, Tertullian linked the Trinity to the economy of salvation. He said: "God's own inner nature...existed before the foundation of the world, until the Son was begotten. For before everything, God was alone, being in himself, for himself, his own world, his own place and all things."[5] Tertullian clarifies this by suggesting that the Word of God was latent in God as the reason of God.[6] God's first creative act was to bring forth his Word so that through his Word he might create the universe. In this way God not only took the form of Son, but the Son "makes God his Father by proceeding from him".[7]

## Heretics?

Looking back we can see that certain views were not what we now understand to be orthodox. But we should be careful about labelling people "heretics". A heretic is someone who "thinks differently"; that is, someone who rejects orthodoxy. But the church fathers

5. Tertullian, *Against Praxeas*, 5.
6. Tertullian, *Against Praxeas*, 5.
7. Tertullian, *Against Praxeas*, 6.

did their theology at a time when orthodoxy was developing. They were not so much heretics as people who took what proved to be wrong turnings on the road to orthodoxy. We should look back on them with great humility. Working on our own, most of us would get no further than the foothills of the mountains they were attempting to climb. The fact that we can label certain views "unorthodox" is only because of a thousand-year process of claim and counter-claim, of clarification and re-clarification.

Tertullian went further, arguing that human history could be divided into the age of the Father (creation and Old Testament), the age of the Son (the incarnation) and the age of the Spirit (post-Pentecost). These were not successive ages. All three are at work in the lives of believers, with the Spirit extending the work already begun by the Father and Son. Tertullian did not reject earlier stages of revelation (unlike Marcion who rejected the God of the Old Testament), but he did believe that the age of the Spirit might produce its own contribution to the canon of Scripture.

**Monarchianism and modalism**
Monarchianism was a movement that taught the undivided rule (monarchy) of God in a strictly monotheistic way.

Some monarchianists maintained the unity of God by denying the divinity of Christ. Jesus was just a man indwelt by God's power.

Others brought together the deity of the Son and unity of God by saying that the Son and the Spirit were different modes of God's existence. One divine being acted sometimes as Father, sometimes as Son and sometimes as Spirit. In effect, the Son is the Father. The unity of God is achieved by sacrificing the threeness of God. The nineteenth-century theologian Adolf von Harnack coined the phrase "modalism" to describe this approach to the doctrine of God.

Tertullian's great work on the Trinity is called *Against Praxeas* and Praxeas seems to have been an early advocate of modalism in Rome. According to Praxeas, it was the Father who became incarnate in the Son and who suffered on the cross – an idea known as "patripassionism" (the suffering of the Father). Praxeas also opposed Montanism, a kind of hyper-charismatic prophetic sect to which Tertullian was attracted. This led to Tertullian's claim that "Praxeas managed two pieces of the devil's business at Rome: he drove out prophecy and brought in heresy. He put flight to the Paraclete and crucified the Father."

Modalism is particularly associated with Sabellius who operated in Rome at the beginning of the third century and, until von Harnack, modalism was generally known as Sabellianism. Sabellius refined the modalism of Praxeas by arguing that the one God contained within himself a double-principle – the Son-Father. This principle was held in tension, but was capable of separation which is what happened on the cross. Although this avoided the charge of patripassionism, it still did not adequately account for the dialogues between the Father and the Son in the Gospels. Sabellius was eventually excommunicated. But modalism has been a particular danger to the Western tradition of theology which tends to make the unity of God its starting point.

Tertullian was forced to refine his position in response to Praxeas. We only know about Praxeas from Tertullian's response to him, but he seems to have argued that the distinctions between the persons of the Trinity are not real. They simply describe the different roles of the one God: the Father is God as Creator, the Son is God as Redeemer and the Spirit is God as Sanctifier. In response, Tertullian pointed to the numerous texts in the New Testament that speak of the Son as a person distinct from the Father, especially those which describe a dialogue between the Father and Son.

---

### Sorting out the terminology

One of the struggles in developing the doctrine of the Trinity was to find a common language that appropriately expressed both the oneness and threeness of God. Tertullian used the Latin terms *persona* (person) to speak of the threeness and *substantia* (substance or being) to speak of the oneness, although his use of *substantia* varied. Today we use "person" of an individual with a unique consciousness and emotions in a way that might imply three gods. But the word *persona* originally meant the mask worn by an actor and therefore the dramatic role or character. This sense of the word is still with us in the term *dramatis personae* to describe a list of characters in play. By Tertullian's time *persona* had also acquired a legal connotation as an objective individual capable of owning property or substance (*substantia*).

While Tertullian was coining the Latin terms *persona* and *substantia*, Origen used the Greek terms *hypostasis* (person) and *ousia* (substance or being). The problem was that, while in Greek you could use *hypostatis* to translate *persona*, the true Latin equivalent of *hypostatis* was *substantia*. Indeed *hypostatis* was commonly used interchangeably with *ousia* (substance or essence). So the word *hypostatis* that some people used to express the threeness of God could also be used to express the one being of God. To avoid the confusion of *substantia* and *hypostatis*, Augustine preferred *essentia* (essence) as a translation of *ousia*. And, while Augustine used the term *persona* as an equivalent of *hypostatis*, he did so with some hesitation. Augustine himself spoke of "modes of being" which sounds like modalism, but was in fact Augustine's attempt to bring out the objective permanence of the three. After Augustine's death, the Council of Chalcedon in AD 451 declared that the Greek word *hypostatis* and the Latin word *persona* should be considered synonymous.

Today the word "person" has become synonymous with individuality and individuality is often defined as being different and separate from others. The persons of the Trinity are not persons in this sense, for that would imply there are three gods. But neither are they simply different masks worn by God, for that would imply modalism. The "persons" are distinct entities sharing one divine being and defined by their relationships with one another.

Augustine said: "When the question is asked, What three? human language labours altogether under great poverty of speech. The answer, however, is given, three 'persons', not that it might be (completely) spoken, but that it might not be left (wholly) unspoken."[8]

In response to Praxeas, Tertullian described the Son and the Spirit as distinct from the Father yet sharing his essence. This was a step forward. But for Tertullian the Father was God in a way which was not true of the Son

---

8. Augustine, *On the Trinity*, 5.9.

and the Spirit. The Son and Spirit share the divine substance because they came from the one God as his agents. The Son and the Spirit were "portions" of the first person of the Trinity. He spoke of the sun with its light and rays; the source that produces a river and canal; the root, shoot and fruit which are one plant. As "portions" of the Father, the Son and the Spirit are therefore in some sense inferior however much the Father might share his power with them, although Tertullian says this inferiority is one of status rather than quality.

---

**Origen**

Origen (c.185–c.254) was born in Alexandria. In 202 his father was martyred. Origen urged his father to remain true to Christ in the face of death. It is even said that Origen himself sought martyrdom and was only stopped because his mother hid his clothes. Origen became a teacher in the catechetical school in Alexandria where those seeking baptism were taught. But he fell out with the Bishop of Alexandria and moved to Caesarea in Palestine. In later life he was tortured for his faith, but refused to recant. Although released, he died a few years later from his injuries.

Origen had a thorough knowledge of Greek philosophy and its influence on his thought has made him a controversial figure. In the sixth century he was condemned as a heretic. Much of his writing consists of biblical exposition following an allegorical method of interpretation which purported to uncover hidden meanings in the text. This allowed him to evade the literal meaning of passages that seemed incompatible with the sophistication of Greek culture. His aim, however, was always to be loyal to the apostolic witness. But Origen also believed Christians had freedom to move beyond the Apostles where they were silent.

Origen describes how Jesus ransomed us from the devil through the cross, but he thinks this is a doctrine for the uneducated. For him salvation involves being deified by looking beyond the earthly Jesus to the eternal Word of God – an idea that his opponents said owed more to Gnosticism than biblical Christianity. Nevertheless, his ideas proved extremely influential in the Eastern tradition of Christianity.

Origen, a theologian based in the Eastern, Greek-speaking half of the Roman Empire, moved beyond economic trinitarianism by insisting that the threeness of God was part of God's eternal being. The term "Son" does not imply a moment of generation. Instead the Son was *eternally* begotten. Origen's formula of three persons or personifications of a single divine essence became very influential.

Origen went on to arrange the Trinity in hierarchical order. Only the Father is God-in-himself (*autotheos*). The Son is his exact image and the Spirit is the image of the Son. So the Son and Spirit have a source which the Father does not have. They are divine except for the attribute of being without beginning. The Son is "God" or "second God", but only the Father is "*the* God". So in Origen, and the Eastern tradition which he influenced, there is a strong sense of subordination within the Trinity. For Origen, the Son and the Spirit are not God in the same way that the Father is.

Nevertheless, by speaking of the Son as eternally begotten, Origen ruled out any modalism. The Trinity we see in the economy of salvation is not a temporary way for God to be God. It reflects in some way God as he is in eternity – what is known as "the immanent Trinity". The Trinity does not just describe God's acts. It also describes God's being.

## Of one substance

A generation after Origen, Arius, a teacher from Alexandria in Egypt, sparked one of the most troublesome conflicts in the first millennium of the church. Origen had said that the Son was co-eternal with the Father and subordinate to him. Arius said you could not have both subordination and co-eternity since co-eternity implies equality. So he ditched co-eternity. Arius took the subordination of Origen a step further, placing the Son on the side of creation rather than the Creator. For Arius, being begotten of the Father meant the Son was created by the Father. So only the Father is the true God. Arius could point to the economic trinitarianism of the second century in support of his argument.

---

**Neoplatonism**

Platonism is the philosophy associated with the Greek philosopher Plato (c.429–346 BC). Platonism enjoyed something of a revival during the third–sixth centuries AD in what became known as Neoplatonism.

One feature of Platonism is its belief in "forms". The world as we experience it is in a state of imperfect flux. But hidden behind this changing world are unchanging "forms". Any person or object is an embodiment or personification (*hypostates*) of its universal form. So, for example, there is an ideal notion of whiteness to which all actual white objects correspond. In the same way there is a form of humanity independent of actual human persons and of which all human persons are imperfect copies. It is like the common mould from which each individual is cast.

Origen was heavily influenced by Neoplatonism. One of its leading figures, Plotinus (c.205–270), was a contemporary of Origen in Alexandria. Origen believed that a being (*ousia*) with one personification (*hypostatis*) could reproduce itself as a second or third person. In the case of the divine being these persons would be the same in every respect expect that the second and third would have a cause (making the first person superior). Arius, however, was an Aristotelian. Aristotle (c.384–322 BC) emphasised the reality of the world as we perceive it and which we can know through observation. Arius believed that if an object reproduced itself then the reproduction had to be a different being (*ousia*). So for Origen it was straightforward to say that the persons of the Trinity could share the same being. But for Arius the persons of the Trinity must be different beings.

Arius' views brought him into conflict with the Bishop of Alexandria. The Bishop's counter-claim was "always the Father, always the Son". In other words, the Father has always existed and the Son has always existed. Eventually Arius was excommunicated in Alexandria, but by now he had gained a wider audience and the controversy became a matter of fierce debate across the Empire. So, when the Emperor Constantine gained control of the Eastern Empire in AD 324, he convened a council at Nicaea to resolve the issue. Constantine had converted to Christianity after seeing, it is claimed, a vision of Christ before a battle. Christianity was sanctioned by the state and soon given special privileges. But Constantine wanted a unified religion for a unified empire.

At the Council of Nicaea Arius was defeated – partly by theological arguments and partly through politics. The resulting Nicene Creed continues to be an important statement of Christian orthodoxy. The form commonly used today is, strictly speaking, the Niceno-Constantinopolitan Creed, since additions were made to the original creed at the Second Ecumenical Council at Constantinople in AD 381.

> We believe in one God, the Father, the Almighty, maker of heaven and earth, of all that is, seen and unseen.
> We believe in one Lord, Jesus Christ, the only Son of God, eternally begotten of the Father, God from God, light from light, true God from true God, begotten, not made, of one Being with the Father; through him all things were made. For us and for our salvation he came down from heaven, was incarnate of the Holy Spirit and the Virgin Mary and became truly human. For our sake he was crucified under Pontius Pilate; he suffered death and was buried. On the third day he rose again in accordance with the Scriptures; he ascended into heaven and is seated at the right hand of the Father. He will come again in glory to judge the living and the dead, and his kingdom will have no end.
> We believe in the Holy Spirit, the Lord, the giver of life, who proceeds from the Father [and the Son], who with the Father and the Son is worshipped and glorified, who has spoken through the prophets. We believe in one holy catholic and apostolic Church. We acknowledge one baptism for the forgiveness of sins. We look for the resurrection of the dead, and the life of the world to come. Amen.

The Nicene Creed took an existing credal statement from the Eastern church and added anti-Arian statements:

- "eternally begotten of the Father" – Arius said that there was a time before Christ was begotten;
- "true God from true God" – Arius said that only the Father was the true God;
- "begotten, not made" – Arius said that begotten meant that Christ had been made by the Father;
- "of one Being (*homoousios*) with the Father".

As a non-Scriptural term, *homoousios* was the most controversial statement at the Council. It means "the same substance" or "consubstantial". It simultaneously maintained the equality of the Father and Son (they are one substance) and the distinction of the Father and Son (since you would not speak of being of one substance with oneself).

---

**Athanasius**

Athanasius (c.297–373) was educated in Alexandria and became an assistant of the Bishop of Alexandria, accompanying him to the Council of Nicaea. When the Bishop died, Athanasius became Bishop and also took on the mantle of the church's chief opponent to Arian ideas. He was Bishop for 46 years until his death. As the Arian controversy raged backwards and forwards, however, Athanasius endured five periods of exile totalling 17 years for his implacable opposition to any compromise.

---

The Arian controversy, however, did not go away with the Council of Nicaea. From exile Arius continued to influence many church and political leaders. In AD 335 Arius met Constantine with a view to resolving the debate, but died shortly afterwards. Even after his death, support for Arius' ideas continued to surface and after the Council of Nicaea the term *homoousios* ("same substance") was widely dropped in favour of a compromise term *homoiousios* ("similar substance"). Athanasius, the new Bishop of Alexandria, stood almost alone against this move. In time he was supported by the Western churches and eventually won the day. At the same time, a debate about the Spirit began. Again Athanasius was in the forefront of the debate, arguing that the Spirit was divine, equal with the Father and Son, and worthy of receiving our worship. "Athanasius taught that in God one and the same identical 'substance' or object, without any division, substitution, or differentiation of content, is permanently presented in three distinct objective forms."[9] Athanasius was not simply belligerent. For Athanasius it was crucial that the Son is co-eternal and equal with the Father. The divinity of Christ matters because only God could restore corrupted humanity.

Arius said you could not have both subordination and co-eternity and so he ditched co-eternity. Athanasius ditched subordination by making a distinction between the "economic Trinity" (the Trinity in relation to creation) and the "immanent Trinity" (the Trinity as it is in itself). Athanasius acknowledged that the Son was subordinate to the Father in the incarnation. The Son does the will of him who sent him. But Athanasius insisted that the Son was not subordinate to God in his being. Subordination is a matter of will rather than to do with the Son's being. The acts of God point to the being of God. But we cannot reduce the being of God to his acts. In his freedom the Son wills to be obedient to the Father and in his freedom the Spirit wills to glorify the Son. But this does not mean the nature of the Son and Spirit is less divine.

This was not some academic disagreement involving ivory-towered theologians. The whole Empire was swept up into the debate. At stake, as Athanasius was quick to point out and as we shall see in Chapter 9, was the eternal salvation of humanity.

---

9. G. L. Prestige, *God in Patristic Thought* (Heinemann, 1936), p. xxix.

# Chapter 6

# Starting with three, starting with one (4th–16th centuries AD)

*In the first millennium AD two Christian traditions developed. The Eastern tradition started with the threeness of God, seeing the Father as the fountainhead of the Trinity with the Son and Spirit deriving their divinity from him. The Western tradition started with the one God, defining the three persons by their eternal relations. The Protestant Reformation focused on the role of the persons of the Trinity in creation and salvation rather than on their eternal being. John Calvin spoke of each of the divine persons as God-in-himself, making them clearly distinct without making one subordinate to the other.*

## The Eastern tradition: Starting with three persons...

During the first centuries after Christ, Christianity gradually developed two broad traditions along linguistic and cultural lines. One was the tradition of the Western Empire where the language was Latin, while in the East the main language was Greek. Each had its own styles, concerns and emphases. The East was influenced by its interaction with the Greek philosophy of Platonism, while the West was influenced by the legal system of Rome. Origen was foundational to the Eastern tradition, while Tertullian was significant to the Western tradition. In 330 the Roman Emperor, Constantine, moved his capital from Rome to Byzantium in the East, renaming it Constantinople (modern-day Istanbul). When in 395 the Roman Empire was formally divided into two Western and Eastern Empires, these differing traditions took political shape. In 476 the Western Empire was overrun by invaders from the north. The Eastern Empire or the Byzantine Empire continued for another thousand years, until it was overrun by the Turks in 1453 who established the Ottoman Empire which continued in power until the end of the First World War.

## The Cappadocian Fathers

The so-called "Cappadocian Fathers" (or "the Three Hierarchs" as they are known in Eastern Orthodoxy) were Basil of Caesarea (c.329–379), his friend Gregory of Nazianzus (c.329–390) and Basil's younger brother, Gregory of Nyssa (c.330–395). All were from noble families in the Roman province of Cappadocia in modern-day Turkey. Basil set up a monastic community on his family's lands and was joined by his brother and Gregory of Nazianzus, whom he had met as a student in Athens. But Basil was drawn into an ecclesiastical career, eventually becoming Bishop of Caesarea in 370. He devoted himself to fight against Arianism, particularly after the death of Athanasius. Gregory of Nazianzus became Bishop of the Nicene party in Constantinople and played a leading role in defending Nicene orthodoxy in the Council of Constantinople. Gregory of Nyssa also became a bishop at his brother's insistence. He was deposed and replaced by an Arian for some years, but returned and remained Bishop of Nyssa for the remainder of his life. All three were heavily influenced by Origen. Basil and Gregory of Nazianzus compiled a selection of Origen's writings known as the *Philokalia*.

One of the great contributions of the Cappadocians was to establish the divinity of the Spirit. Basil wrote a work *On the Holy Spirit* which defends the worship of the Spirit. But, although Basil clearly accepts the deity of the Spirit in his letters, for political reasons the treatise stops short of affirming that the Spirit is of one substance with the Father. Gregory of Nazianzus, however, explicitly argues this in his five *Theological Orations*. The Spirit must either be God or a creature, he argues, and only his full divinity can give coherence to Christian theology.

After Origen, a major influence on the Eastern tradition has been the work of a group of theologians known as the Cappadocian Fathers: Basil of Caesarea, Gregory of Nazianzus and Gregory of Nyssa. The Cappadocians opposed any notion that the Trinity could be seen as one person expanding into three. God is one substance of which there are three persons. The one and the three exist in eternity. The difference, they said, between "substance" and "person" is the difference between universals and particulars – an idea influenced by Neoplatonism. For example, every person shares a common humanity (the universal) while having his or her own distinguishing characteristics that define him or her as an individual (a particular). In the same way, the Cappadocians argued, the Trinity consists of the common substance of deity with each divine person having his own distinguishing features. Basil and Gregory of Nyssa said:

> Substance relates to person as universal relates to particular. Each of us shares in existence through the common substance and yet is a specific individual because of his own characteristics. So also with God, substance refers to that which is common, like goodness,

deity or other attributes, while person is seen in the special characteristics of fatherhood, sonship or sanctifying power.[1]

Peter, James and John are called three humans, even though they share a single common humanity... So how do we compromise our belief by saying on the one hand that the Father, Son and the Holy Spirit have a single godhead, while on the other hand denying that we are talking about three gods?[2]

At first sight this seems to lay the Cappadocians open to the charge of tritheism: if substance and person relate like humanity and individuals then there must surely be three individual gods. But the Cappadocians refuted this charge. Gregory of Nyssa wrote a work called *That We Should Not Think of Saying There Are Three Gods*. While three men may pursue activities separately, in God each act is common to all three. The Cappadocians argued that in each divine person the essence of the one God is fully manifest. To see God is to see all three persons. Developing an idea from Athanasius,[3] they said each person of the Trinity shares the life of the other two so that they mutually interpenetrate each other in a community of being. They share, as it were, the same space. A later anonymous theologian used the Greek word "perichoresis" or "co-inherence" to express this idea. The idea of perichoresis enabled the Cappadocians to affirm the unity of God without compromising the distinction of persons. Each person of the Trinity is a complete manifestation of the divine being.

The Cappadocians continued to define the distinction between the divine persons in terms of the *cause* that had brought each person into being (though it is hard for us to imagine how the word "cause" can apply to an eternal

---

1. Basil of Caesarea, *Letter*, 214.4.
2. Cited in Alister McGrath, *Christian Theology: An Introduction* (Blackwell, 3rd ed., 2001), p. 331.
3. See T. F. Torrance, *The Trinitarian Faith* (T&T Clark, 1988), pp. 302–313.

being). The Cappadocians turned the processes of begetting and proceeding into attributes. The Father has "unbegottenness", the Son had "begottenness" and the Spirit has "procession". Like Origen, the Cappadocians believed that the nature of God is personified in the person of the Father. But whereas Origen saw the Father as the first in a series of three (Father-Son-Spirit), the Cappadocians believed the Spirit proceeded directly from the Father. To distinguish the Son and the Spirit, Gregory of Nyssa said the Spirit proceeded *from* the Father *through* the Son. But the Cappadocians would not accept that the Spirit proceeded from the Son – that would be to admit two principles of origin within God. They acknowledged that the difference between eternal begetting and eternal procession was a mystery. But they were careful, nevertheless, to maintain this distinction. The Spirit is not a second Son and therefore not an alternative mediator.

The work of the Cappadocian Fathers has shaped the Eastern tradition up to this day. The Father is the fountainhead of the God. He personifies his divine essence in the Son and the Spirit so that their divinity is derived from his, albeit through an eternal act. The differences between the persons are defined by their causal relations – the Father is the cause of the Son and the Spirit. So the Eastern tradition has tended to start with the Father, and accounts for the Son and the Spirit as persons eternally caused by the Father. It thus starts with the threeness of God and move towards definitions of his unity. This is reflected in its icons, which often express the Trinity as three people in conversation. It is reflected, too, in its baptismal practice in which a believer is submerged under the water three times corresponding to each person of the Trinity. From a Western perspective, the danger of Eastern trinitarianism has been a tendency towards subordination or even tritheism.

## The Western tradition: Starting with one God...

The teaching of the Cappadocian Fathers was translated into Latin by Hilary of Poitiers (c.315–368) and influenced the Western tradition. But, in the West, trinitarian thought took a different turn. Western theology tends to start with the one God and work towards defining the threeness of God. As a result, the West has faced the opposite danger of that faced by the East. Western theology has had a tendency towards modalism in which the unity of God overwhelms the threeness of God.

### Augustine

Augustine (354–430) was born in what is now Algeria. His mother was a devout Christian and from an early age he was sent to catechesis (a sort of early Sunday school). But when he went away to study in Carthage he took a mistress and by the time he was eighteen had a son. Augustine moved to Rome to continue his career and ended up as Public Orator in Milan where he enjoyed the fine rhetoric of the local Bishop, Ambrose. Gradually he became intrigued by the message and was thrown into a period of spiritual crisis. While wrestling with his conscience in a garden, he heard a child singing "pick up and read". Augustine took this as a message from God to read the Bible and started at Romans 13:13–14. Augustine wrote later: "I neither wished nor needed to read further... it was as if a light of relief from all anxiety flooded into my heart. All the shadows of doubt were dispelled."[4] He gave up his career for an aesthetic life of study. In 391, however, he was press-ganged into the priesthood on a visit to Hippo (also in modern Algeria) and five years later

---

4. Augustine, *Confessions*, VIII, xii [30].

was made Bishop, which he remained until his death. Augustine made a major contribution to Christian thought in a number of areas including the Trinity.

While Augustine drew on the Cappadocian Fathers, he began as Tertullian had done with the oneness of God. The essence of God was primary over the persons. Augustine was influenced by a different branch of Neoplatonism to that which influenced the Cappadocians, although Augustine's dependence on Neoplatonism is much debated. Marius Victorinus (died c.360), a converted philosopher, said that the being of God is movement. God is a dynamic being rather than a static being. The eternal origin of the second and third persons of the Trinity seems to support this idea. Augustine developed this by arguing that God is perfectly conscious of his eternal state of being. He equated this perfect self-knowledge with the divine Word. To this Augustine added a third principle, that of love. Love united the being of God with its self-knowledge.

So far the trinitarian debate had been about causal relationships. Augustine did not deny the credal formulations to which this approach had led, but he started instead with the trinitarian *relationships*. What defines the trinitarian persons is not the causal relations of begetting and procession, but the loving relationships within the godhead. The three persons are differentiated through their relationships with one another. The Father loves the Son, the Son loves the Father and the Spirit is the bond of love that unites them. The Father is the Father because he has a Son, and the Son is the Son because he has a Father. The Spirit is the bond of love that exists because the Father and the Son are perfectly related. "I present in my love for anything three things:

myself, what I love, and love itself. I cannot love without loving a lover; for there is no love where nothing is loved. Lover, the loved and love: these are three."[5] This meant that in Augustine's thought the Spirit proceeded from both the Father and the Son. Augustine observed that it is the Spirit who binds us to God. This, argued Augustine, reflects the role of the Spirit in binding the Father and the Son.

The strength of Augustine's formulation is that it "discarded the last vestiges of economic trinitarianism and stressed the full, eternal co-equality of the persons".[6] The weakness is its tendency to depersonalise the Spirit. The relationship between a human Father and Son does not require a third person. It requires love, but love is a quality of persons, not a person itself. For the Cappadocians the unity of the Trinity was located in the Father as the fountainhead of the three. Gregory of Nyssa says: "The three have one nature (that is, God), the ground of their unity being the Father."[7] In Augustine the unity of the Trinity was located in the Spirit.

Augustine looked for analogies to help us understand what faith believes. God left his imprint on his creation especially in humanity, Augustine argues. And, perhaps under the influence of Neoplatonism, Augustine believes the high point of humanity is the human mind and so this is where he looks for analogies. The mind consists of memory, understanding and love (or will). These three faculties are distinct, but together make one mind in such a way as one cannot exist apart from the others. These "psychological analogies" feature prominently in Augustine's discussion of the Trinity, although he recognises their limitations.

---

5. Augustine, *On the Trinity*, 9.2.
6. Gerald Bray, "The Patristic Dogma" in Peter Toon and James D. Spiceland (eds), *One God in Trinity* (Samuel Bagster, 1980), p. 59.
7. Cited in Alister McGrath, *Christian Theology*, p. 331.

Augustine's ideas were developed by Richard of St Victor in the twelfth century. Richard was part of a group of theologians and mystical writers known as the Victorines because they were part of the staff of the Abbey Church of St Victor in Paris, where they lived as an ascetic community. Like Augustine, Richard saw God as the supreme expression of love. But whereas Augustine's focus on the human mind gave his trinitarianism an individualistic slant, Richard saw them as a community of interrelating persons united in love. The infinite love of God must always have had an infinite object. And, argued Richard, love must have a third party otherwise it is self-indulgent. True love is to desire that the beloved should be loved by another. So the Father and Son desire to share their love with another – the Holy Spirit.[8] Richard went further, seeing the Trinity as a model of human society. This so-called social model of the Trinity has received renewed interest in recent years as a model for holding together unity and diversity in our increasingly pluralist societies.

---

**Thomas Aquinas**
Thomas Aquinas (1225–1274) was the son of the Count of Aquino from Roccasecca, near Naples in Italy. As a young man he joined the new Dominican order of monks. His family, who wanted him to join the more prestigious Benedictine order, held him hostage for several months. But Aquinas stood firm and was eventually sent by Dominicans to study in Paris. After his studies he spent the rest of his life teaching theology in France and Italy. His influence on theology, especially Roman Catholic theology, is immense even to this day.

---

8. For a modern development of this idea see David Coffey, Deus Trinitas: *The Doctrine of the Triune God* (OUP, 1999).

The tendency in the Western tradition to start with the unity of God and only then account for the plurality of the Trinity reaches its fullest form in the influential medieval theologian, Thomas Aquinas. In the first three chapters of *Summa Contra Gentiles (Against the Heathen)* Aquinas argues on the basis of reason and philosophy alone. Using reason in this way Aquinas claims to establish the existence of God, his attributes, creation, providence and predestination. The Trinity, however, is left along with the incarnation, the sacraments and the resurrection until book four, which deals with doctrines that can only be known through revelation. Reason, argued Aquinas, can demonstrate the unity of God's essence, but not the distinctiveness of the persons. Even then what is said about the distinctiveness of the persons must fit what we know by reason. Aquinas says that God acts in two ways: by understanding and by willing. The distinctiveness of the persons is determined by these two acts. The Son is defined by an intellectual act of generation – the Father reproduces the Word in his likeness. The Spirit is an act of divine will – in his love God wills to bring forth something which is different from himself. This act is perfect and so the result is fully divine. Aquinas used the terms "paternity", "filiation" and "procession" to describe the different persons.

Arguably the result is a philosophical and abstract trinitarianism that does not do justice to the relational nature of the divine persons revealed in Scripture. Nevertheless, Aquinas' approach has had a huge impact on the Western tradition. Aquinas discussed the one God, and then, having established God's unity, dealt with the triunity of God. Typically, subsequent Western systematic theologies have followed this pattern, discussing the unity of God, then his attributes and only then the Trinity. As a result, the Trinity has often been regarded as a secondary doctrine. The oneness of God has been seen as primary and foundational, sometimes creating a unitarian mindset.

## East and West move apart

In 1054 Cardinal Humbert went into the cathedral of Constantinople. In his hand was a document from Pope Leo IX. He marched up to the altar and slammed it down. As he left the cathedral he symbolically shook the dust off his feet. The Western church had excommunicated the Eastern church. Soon after, the Eastern church returned the compliment!

In the fifth and sixth centuries people in the West had started adding the phrase *filioque* – "and from the Son" – to the part of the Nicene Creed which spoke of the procession of the Holy Spirit: "We believe in the Holy Spirit, the Lord, the giver of life, who proceeds from the Father *and from the Son.*" The original creed, agreed at Nicaea in 325, had simply affirmed belief "in the Holy Spirit". The Second Ecumenical Council in Constantinople in 381 amplified the Nicene Creed, adding the affirmation that the Spirit is "the Lord, the giver of life who proceeds from the Father", but without a reference to the Son. *Filioque* seems to have been added first at a local council in Toledo in 589. Over time it gained widespread acceptance in the West and was officially sanctioned in 1017. But it has always been rejected by the Eastern tradition.

Exegetically the issue revolved round the words of Jesus in John 15:26: "When the Counsellor comes, whom I will send to you from the Father, the Spirit of truth who goes out from the Father, he will testify about me." This was the proof text for the Eastern tradition. The Spirit goes out (proceeds) from the Father alone. But Western theologians emphasised the sending by the Son. They also placed John 14:26 alongside 15:26: "But the Counsellor, the Holy Spirit, whom the Father will send in my name...." Read together in this way, they argued, it is clear that both the Father and the Son sent the Spirit for the sake of the other. Augustine also pointed to John 20:22 where Jesus breathes on his disciples, saying "Receive the Holy Spirit."

But the issue went beyond the interpretation of Scripture. In the Eastern tradition the Father was the fountainhead of the godhead, its eternal cause and the source of its divine being. To say that the Spirit proceeded from the Son was to say that there were two fountain-heads in the godhead, two causes and even two divine beings. They acknowledged a secondary sense in which the Son was the source of the Spirit, but expressed this as "*from* the Father *through* the Son".

The Western tradition, however, did not identify the divine being with the Father. There was one God subsist-ing in three persons who equally shared the divine being. The difference between the divine persons was not defined by causal relations as it was in the East, but by personal relations. In the East the begetting of the Son by the Father indicated an eternal cause. In the West it indi-cated an eternal relationship. This relationship could be expressed in the principle of non-identity: the Son is the Son because the Son is not the Father and he is not the Spirit. It was thus important for the Spirit to relate to the others in a different way. If the Spirit proceeded from the Father alone then the Son and the Spirit could not be dis-tinguished. They would be, as it were, two sons. Only a double procession of the Spirit from the Father *and* the Son would establish the distinctiveness of the Spirit. So they thought the *filioque* clause was important to main-tain the distinctions between the trinitarian persons. The Cappadocian Fathers had recognised this problem and insisted on a distinction between "begetting" and "pro-ceeding", without identifying what this distinction involved.

The Eastern theologians were trying to find a satis-factory way of stating the unity of God because their starting point was the threeness of the persons. They located the unity of God in the Father as the sole cause of the Son and the Spirit. Meanwhile, in the West, theolo-gians were trying to find a satisfactory way of stating the distinctions of the persons because their starting point was the unity of the divine essence. The Son and the Spirit could not be replicas of each other as they appeared to be if derived from the Father in the same way. To the East, Western theology contained within it a tendency towards modalism – the equality of the three tending to become the sameness of the three. To the West, Eastern theology involved a continuing tendency towards subordination with the essence of God associated with the Father alone, although this tendency is mitigated by the idea of peri-choresis.

The dispute over the *filioque* clause was the formal reason for the schism between East and West in 1054 that led to separate Eastern Orthodox and Roman Catholic churches. But there were other factors at play. Although the issue had been hotly debated, it did not become schis-matic until the Pope in Rome tried to impose *filioque* on the East. This was a step too far. For one thing, while they were happy to honour the Pope, Eastern Christians did not accept the supremacy of papal authority. For another thing, they thought of themselves – with some justifica-tion – as the sophisticated theologians of the Christian world. In reality the formal separation of 1054 was one event in a process. The two traditions had been growing apart over a period of time. And good relationships con-tinued between the two sides after 1054. The split deep-ened in 1204 when Constantinople, the capital of the Eastern Empire, was ransacked by Western crusaders. An unsuccessful attempt at compromise was made in Florence in 1439. And the matter was left unresolved after the Eastern Empire fell to the Turks in 1453. Only in 1965 did the two sides formally rescind their mutual excommunication of each other, albeit without resolving the *filioque* debate.

## East and West coming together: The Reformation

### The Reformation

On 31 October 1517 a young monk named Martin Luther nailed a piece of paper with 95 theses to the church door at Wittenberg, Germany. The document attacked the church's preoccupation with material wealth. The local Archbishop complained to the Pope, but the opposition only made Luther more resolute. He was finally excommunicated in 1521. By now, though, Luther's ideas were spreading across Europe. Central to this movement was Luther's rediscovery of justification by faith – the truth that we are made right with God through faith in Christ's work and not through our good works. Luther's actions precipitated a theological revolution with major political implications. It represented a return to biblical Christianity. Many of the truths which appear commonplace to evangelicals today were hammered out during the Reformation.

One of the core principles of the Protestant Reformation was *sola Scriptura* – Scripture alone. The Reformers said that the Bible was the only true authority for the believer – not the Pope or the church or tradition. This meant that, though the Reformers were resolutely trinitarian, they were wary of the extra-biblical language used to spell out the doctrine. Luther disliked the language of "substance" and "Trinity", but he defended such terms against Reformers like Martin Bucer who wanted to stick to biblical language alone. Luther argued that, while the creeds should not be seen as an alternative authority to the Scriptures, they were useful in protecting the intentions of Scripture from heresy. The great Anabaptist theologian, Menno Simons, wrote a book on the Trinity called *Confession of the Triune God* (1550) in which he sought to set out the doctrine of the Trinity without reference to the creeds and controversies of the past. He believed it could be done simply through an exposition of the Scriptures. In reality, however, he was not entirely able to keep to his own guidelines, using the extra-biblical language of personhood and speaking of the procession of the Holy Spirit. John Calvin shared this distaste for non-biblical terms, but like Luther he recognised they were needed because heretics like Arius had used biblical language to express unbiblical ideas. Speaking of the non-biblical terms he said: "I could wish they were buried, if only among all men this faith were agreed on: that Father and Son and Spirit are one God, yet the Son is not the Father, nor the Spirit the Son, but that they are differentiated by a peculiar quality."[9]

---

**John Calvin**

John Calvin (1509–1564) was born in France and studied for the priesthood in Paris. At some point – the date is not certain – he underwent a sudden conversion. From then on he became committed to the study of the Scriptures and the teachings of the Reformation. He had an unsuccessful period of ministry in Geneva,

---

9. John Calvin, *Institutes*, 1.13.5.

Switzerland, followed by a happier time as a pastor and teacher in Strasburg. Then in 1541 he was invited back to Geneva where he spent the rest of his life, seeking to shape church and society in line with the gospel.

It is often said that the Reformers gave little attention to the doctrine of the Trinity, accepting the received tradition and focusing their attention elsewhere. This view, however, is challenged by Gerald Bray. Such a view, he suspects, arises from historians with little interest in theology and from an ecumenism that plays down the fundamental divides of the Reformation.

> The Protestant Reformers...had a vision of God which was fundamentally different from anything which had gone before, or which has appeared since. The great issues of Reformation theology – justification by faith, election, assurance of salvation – can be properly understood only against the background of a trinitarian theology which gave these matters their peculiar importance...[10]

Bray argues that Calvin in particular took the doctrine of the Trinity in new directions.[11] Calvin argued that if we think of God as anything less than the Trinity we commit idolatry. We cannot start, as Aquinas had done, with the one God and then add on the Trinity. Indeed Calvin argued that the essence of God must be of secondary importance in Christian theology since the Bible only speaks sparingly of it. We are told only of its immensity and spirituality – both attributes, according to Calvin, that should check our imaginations and speculations. The gulf between God's majesty and our sinfulness means we should focus instead on the persons of the Trinity in their gracious work of creation and redemption.

---

10. Gerald Bray, *The Doctrine of God* (IVP, 1993), pp. 197–198.
11. Gerald Bray, *The Doctrine of God*, pp. 199–212.

This means, as Philip Butin argues, that for Calvin "the doctrine of the Trinity *is* the doctrine of God."[12] In other words there can be no understanding of God which is not trinitarian. Everywhere one looks in Calvin we see a trinitarian structure to Christian experience. For example:

> We shall possess a right definition of faith if we call it a firm and certain knowledge of God's benevolence towards us, founded upon the truth of the freely given promise in Christ, both revealed to our minds and sealed upon our hearts through the Holy Spirit.[13]

> All those who, by the kindness of God the Father, through the working of the Holy Spirit, have entered into fellowship with Christ, are set apart as God's property and personal possession.[14]

Calvin asserted that the trinitarian persons were equal to one another in every respect. In a formal sense this was the case in the tradition. The Athanasian Creed from the fourth and fifth centuries said that "none is greater or less than another." But, as we have seen, in practice the Eastern tradition tended to give priority to the Father as the source of divinity, while the Western tradition made the Spirit the bond of unity in the godhead and perhaps therefore the source of divinity. In contrast, Calvin said that each person of the Trinity was "God-in-himself" (*autotheos*). Father, Son and the Holy Spirit are each God in the fullest sense. This contrasted with the Eastern tradition which said only the Father was God-in-himself. It also contrasted with the modalist tendencies in the Western tradition which said none of the three were fully equal to the divine essence. Calvin said the three persons were co-equal in their divinity. Calvin defines a divine person, using a term coined by some medieval theolo-

---

12. Philip W. Butin, "Reformed Ecclesiology: Trinitarian Grace According to Calvin", *Studies in Reformed Theology and History* 2:1 (Princeton Theological Seminary, 1994), p. 6.
13. John Calvin, *Institutes*, 3.2.7.
14. John Calvin, *Institutes*, 4.1.3.

gians, as a "'subsistence' in God's essence, which, while related to the others, is distinguished by an incommunicable quality".[15] By "incommunicable quality" he means a characteristic that the other two do not have. This "incommunicable quality" is their unique relation to the other two. The Father is uniquely the Father through his relation to the Son.

By saying each of the three persons was God-in-himself, Calvin said the relations between them were voluntary. One could not impose his will on another. But this freedom did not lead to anarchy because there was one divine will governed by God's love. Calvin cements the move in the Western tradition away from the notion of causality. Everything the Son does has its beginning in the Father in the sense that it must be understood with reference to the eternal plan of the Father. But the Son is not *caused* by the Father – both are God-in-himself. Calvin rejected the division of labour into Father as Creator, Son as Redeemer and the Spirit as Sanctifier because it was susceptible to modalism. Calvin argued instead that all three persons were involved in creation, redemption and sanctification. Calvin used the idea from the Cappadocians of perichoresis, but focuses it less on the inner life of God and more on his trinitarian activity in creating and redeeming the world. The persons have distinctive roles, but they do not work separately. "To the Father," he said, "is attributed the beginning of action, the fountain and source of all things; to the Son, wisdom, counsel, and arrangement in action, while the energy and efficacy of action is assigned to the Spirit."[16] This maintained the priority of the Father without implying any implications for the being of God. To encounter one person is to know the others. Knowledge of one of the per-

---

15. John Calvin, *Institutes*, 1.13.6.
16. John Calvin, *Institutes*, 1.13.18.

sons involves knowledge of the other two at the same time. In biblical terms, to see Jesus is to know the Father, the Spirit is the Spirit of Christ and so on.

Gerald Bray claims that Calvin was synthesising East and West. The person Calvin attacks most in his discussion of the Trinity is Michael Servetus (1511–1553). Calvin enlarged the section on the Trinity in his major work, *Institutes of the Christian Religion*, in response to an attack by Servetus. Servetus was eventually executed in Geneva for his heretical views. Bray argues that Servetus was propounding a mixture of modalism (the persons are different modes of God's activity) and Arianism (the Son is less than God). The reason Calvin reacted so strongly against Servetus was that he recognised a different attempt to synthesise East and West – one that combined the worst of both. Calvin himself was attempting a more orthodox synthesis of East and West. In common with the Eastern tradition Calvin thought the essence of God was all but unknowable to sinful people. And by speaking of each person of the Trinity as God-in-himself, Calvin affirms with the East the distinctiveness of the persons in the face of Western modalism. But he also affirms with the West the equal status of the persons in the face of Eastern subordinationism. The three are bound together through a common will and a perichoretic life.

In the *Institutes* Calvin quotes from Gregory of Nazianzus from the Eastern tradition: "I cannot think on the one without quickly being circled by the splendour of the three; nor can I discern the three without being straightway carried back to the one."[17]

---

17. Gregory of Nazianzus, *Theological Oration* 40.412; cited by Calvin in *Institutes*, 1.13.17.

# Chapter 7

# At the margins, at the centre (17th–20th centuries AD)

*The Enlightenment, with its emphasis on what could be known through human reason, had little time for the Trinity. It either thought of god as a remote deity or regarded the Trinity as of marginal significance. But the twentieth century has seen renewed interest in the Trinity. There has also been considerable interest in the Trinity as a model for human personhood and social interactions.*

## The doctrine of the Trinity at the margins

### The Enlightenment: An unreasonable doctrine

The doctrine of the Trinity faced new challenges with the movement known as the Enlightenment in the eighteenth and nineteenth centuries. Thinkers disillusioned with Christian orthodoxy began detaching the idea of god from revelation. Belief in god, it was claimed, could be established on rational grounds without the need for revelation. The result was belief in a god quite different from the God of the Bible. The unitarian tendencies of the Western tradition ran to seed in deism and Unitarianism.

### The Enlightenment

The religious wars that followed the Reformation created a desire to find a basis for truth independent of religion. This coincided with scientific advances pioneered by Isaac Newton and the economic progress of the industrial revolution. There was great confidence in what humanity could achieve. In this context René Descartes (1596–1650), in his search for a basis for truth, came up with his famous dictum: *cogito ergo sum* – "I think, therefore I am." We could find a basis for truth in human reason.

Deists believed in a god who was the creator of the universe, but assumed that it did not now intervene in the world. They sought to develop natural religion in which human reason interpreted the patterns of the world bestowed by a deity. The Trinity, however, could not be read from the order of creation. Instead god was seen as a benevolent, but remote being. Christianity was one faith among other legitimate, if inferior, faiths, so a concern for its distinctive understanding of God lessened.

Alongside deism grew Unitarianism. There had always been people who denied the plurality of God, but during the Enlightenment they became a more self-conscious grouping. Early Unitarians were those who did not think the Trinity was taught in the Bible, but later Unitarianism was largely rationalistic. Nature and reason replaced the Scriptures as the ultimate source of theology and trinitarianism was seen as irrational. In the early eighteenth century a number of free-church ministers converted to Unitarianism convictions. At the time, it was viewed as the cutting edge of religion in a new rationalistic age.

Immanuel Kant believed knowledge had to be established on the basis of empirical evidence or rational argument. This, he argued, made confidence in the existence of God impossible. Belief in God and life after death were practical assumptions because they justified living according to moral precepts. But they were assumptions rather than proven truths. As for the Trinity, Kant said: "From the doctrine of the Trinity, taken literally, nothing whatsoever can be gained for practical purposes, even if one believes one comprehends it – and even less if one recognises that it surpassed all our concepts."[1] Albrecht Ritschl, the liberal theologian, rejected the Trinity as impossibly speculative. The Trinity was being marginalised in Western thought.

Another feature of the Enlightenment was a focus on humanity as the proper subject of intellectual study. Alexander Pope summed this up in his dictum: "Know then thyself, presume not God to scan, the proper study of mankind is man." This human-centred approach led to the rise of psychology, sociology and anthropology as academic disciplines. In theology it created a reluctance in biblical studies to go beyond the historical context of the text to make metaphysical statements about God. Jesus the man was thought of as separate from the Christ of faith. The emphasis on the divinity of Christ in John's Gospel, for example, was said to reflect the church's faith rather than the true identity of the historical Jesus. As a result "God becomes a more or less shadowy figure *behind* Jesus rather than the one known through him."[2]

## Romanticism: An irrelevant doctrine

The Romantic movement rejected this emphasis on "cold reason" because it ignored the emotions of the human spirit. Poets like William Blake (1757–1827), William

---

1. Cited in Philip W. Butin, *The Trinity* (Geneva Press, 2001), p. 54.
2. Colin Gunton, *The Promise of Trinitarian Theology* (T&T Clark, 1991), p. 2.

Wordsworth (1770–1850) and Samuel Taylor Coleridge (1772–1834) rejected the mechanical world of rationalism and industrialisation. Instead they believed we would find ultimate truth in humanity's aesthetic and spiritual sensitivities. Although the Romantic movement reacted against the rationalism of the time, it was still part of the Enlightenment. It replaced reason with experience, but it was still about what humanity could know for itself without revelation.

The main representative of Romanticism within theology is the nineteenth-century theologian Friedrich Schleiermacher (1768–1834) – known as the father of theological liberalism. Schleiermacher wanted to make Christianity credible to its "cultured despisers". He identified "a feeling of absolute dependence" as the common human experience, arguing that this expressed a feeling of dependence on God. Schleiermacher placed the doctrine of the Trinity as an appendix at the end of his theology. Although Schleiermacher talked of the Trinity as the "the coping-stone of Christian doctrine",[3] in reality the marginalisation of the Trinity was complete. At best Schleiermacher thought of the Trinity as summarising the union of God with humanity in the personality of Jesus and the Spirit of the church. But this was just a way of describing a psychological experience. Schleiermacher rejected any trinitarian dogma as impossibly speculative and abandoned the credal understandings of the Trinity because he did not accept eternal distinctions within the "Supreme Being".

## Georg Hegel: A symbolic doctrine

At first sight the German philosopher Georg W. F. Hegel (1770–1831) looks like an exception to this marginalisation of the Trinity. He has been called "the philosopher of

---

3. Cited in Philip W. Butin, *The Trinity*, p. 56.

the Trinity".[4] Hegel saw history as a process with a trinitarian structure. History developed through an ongoing dialectical process of thesis, antithesis and synthesis. God or Absolute Spirit (thesis) enters the finite world in the forms of art, science, religion and cultural movements (antithesis), reconciling the world to itself (synthesis). Clearly this has only a passing resemblance to Christian orthodoxy. Hegel saw Christian doctrine as a symbolic way of describing philosophical ideas. Religion, according to Hegel, is the childhood of philosophy. Trinitarian patterns may have been important in Hegel's thought, but the trinitarian God of the Bible is marginal. Despite this, Hegel has been influential on Christian theologians like Jürgen Moltmann.

## The doctrine of the Trinity at the centre

### Karl Barth: God is known through the Trinity

> One day in early August 1914 stands out in my personal memory as a black day. Ninety-three German intellectuals impressed public opinion by their proclamation in support of the war policy of Kaiser Wilhelm II and his counsellors. Among these intellectuals I discovered to my horror almost all of my theological teachers whom I had greatly venerated. In despair over what this indicated about the sign of the times, I suddenly realised that I should no longer follow either their ethics or dogmatics, or their understandings of the Bible and of history. For me at least nineteenth-century theology no longer held any future.[5]

So wrote a young Swiss pastor called Karl Barth. Barth had been educated by some of the leading liberal theologians of the day. But his experience of pastoral ministry had made him acutely aware of the inadequacies of his

---

4. Jürgen Moltmann, *The Future of Creation* (SCM, 1979), p. 82.
5. Cited in Alister McGrath, *A Cloud of Witnesses* (IVP, 1990), p. 113.

training. He had to preach week by week, but found that liberal theology had nothing to say. The support of his former teachers for German militarism was the final straw for Barth. Barth turned instead back to revelation as the starting point of theology, seeing the revelation of God in Christ as a radical "No" to all human reason and endeavour.

---

**Karl Barth**

Karl Barth (1886–1968) was born in Switzerland and educated in Germany. In 1919 he published a commentary of Romans, with a more radical second edition in 1922. It was not a commentary in the usual sense of the word, more a sustained critique of the liberal identification of God with human civilisation. "Let God be God," was Barth's cry. God is radically different from humanity (hence the description "dialectical theology" for Barth's early thought). We are wholly dependent on God's revelation and redemption. Barth's protest proved to have dramatic repercussions in the theological world. Barth described himself as like a man groping around in the dark who grabbed at something and discovered it to be a bell rope whose bell then tolled across Europe. In 1932 Barth published volume one of his major work, *Church Dogmatics*. Thirteen volumes and six million words later it was still unfinished when he died in 1968. It is estimated that, reading eight hours a day, it would take ten months to read it.

---

Hand in hand with Barth's emphasis on revelation was an emphasis on the doctrine of the Trinity. In the preface to the first translation of the first volume of *Church Dogmatics*, G. T. Thomson says this is "undoubtedly the greatest treatise on the Trinity since the

Reformation". In the retranslation G. W. Bromiley and T. F. Torrance extend this claim back to Augustine.[6] The reason for this is not simply the meaning and understanding Barth gives to the Trinity, but the position he gives it. In direct contrast to Schleiermacher, Barth places the Trinity not as an appendix, nor indeed under the doctrine of God, but under the doctrine of the word of God so that the Trinity becomes the basis for theology.

The liberalism of the Enlightenment had turned from divine revelation to human reason and made the Trinity marginal. Barth turned from human reason back to revelation and made the Trinity central. This, as we shall see in the next chapter, is because the Trinity was central to Barth's idea of revelation. Barth saw the Trinity as the Christian response to modernity's scepticism about knowledge of God. Through Jesus, the Father makes himself known in history, and through the Holy Spirit he enables us to recognise this as divine revelation. So Barth spoke of the Trinity as the Revealer (the Father), Revelation (the Son) and Revealedness (the Holy Spirit): "To the same God who in unimpaired unity is the Revealed, the Revelation and the Revealedness, there is also ascribed in unimpaired differentiation within Himself this threefold mode of being."[7] Barth preferred to use "modes of being" to "persons" because the modern use of "person" implies too much distinctiveness. To guard against modalist thinking he emphasised that these are modes of being not modes of activity.

### Karl Rahner: The economic Trinity is the immanent Trinity

Another feature of Barth's trinitarianism has been developed by the influential Catholic theologian, Karl Rahner

---

6. Karl Barth, *Church Dogmatics*, 1.1, p. ix.
7. Karl Barth, *Church Dogmatics*, 1.1, p. 299.

(1904–1984). Barth said that the revelation of God in Christ is not different from God's true self. In other words, the economic Trinity (God in relation to the world) mirrors the immanent Trinity (God in himself). Rahner lamented the marginalisation of the Trinity, complaining that in practice many believers are not much more than monotheists. Rahner insists that what God does in the world fully corresponds to who God is. The God who interacts with the world as Father, Son and Spirit is trinitarian in his being. Rahner used the following axiom: "The economic Trinity is the immanent Trinity and the immanent Trinity is the economic Trinity."[8] Rahner's intention here is important. He was trying to rescue the doctrine of the Trinity from metaphysical speculation isolated from the rest of theology. He wanted to root the doctrine of the Trinity in the Bible story so that it was linked to Christian salvation and worship.

Nevertheless Rahner's identification of the immanent and economic Trinity requires some qualification.[9] If there is no distinction at all between them then we may return to the economic trinitarianism of the second and third centuries in which the divine persons are reduced to different modes of activity in the history of salvation. Or we may make God's involvement in the world necessary for his being. A distinction between the immanent and economic Trinity protects the freedom of God's grace. Rahner, for example, sees the eternal *processions* within God (the Son begotten of the Father, the Spirit proceeding from the Father and the Son) as the same as the *missions* of God (the sending of the Son by the Father, the sending of the Spirit by the Father and the Son). But this risks making God's actions towards the world a necessity of his

---

8. Karl Rahner, *The Trinity* (Burns & Oates, 1970), p. 21.
9. Ralph Del Colle, "The Triune God" in Colin E. Gunton (ed.), *The Cambridge Companion to Christian Doctrine* (CUP, 1997), pp. 136–137.

being rather than acts of grace. God did not have to become the economic Trinity, but did so freely in love. So on the one hand, God's immanent being is not different from the economic Trinity. There are not two trinities – one in eternity and another relating to the world. On the other hand, the immanent Trinity cannot be reduced to the economic Trinity.

## *Jürgen Moltmann: The Trinity is open to humanity*

Barth and Rahner's concern to place the Trinity at the centre of theology is shared by three other prominent twentieth-century German theologians: Jürgen Moltmann (b. 1926), Eberhard Jüngel (b. 1934) and Wolfgang Pannenberg (b. 1928). Jüngel roots his understanding of the Trinity in the cross while Pannenberg provides an eschatological perspective on the Trinity. We will focus on the work of Moltmann who does both, providing an eschatological perspective on the Trinity rooted in the cross and resurrection.

Moltmann believes that the cross and the Trinity mutually interpret one another.[10] The cross, says Moltmann, "divides God from God to the utmost degree of enmity and distinction".[11] The Son suffers abandonment by the Father, but the Father also suffers, albeit in a different way, for he suffers the loss of his Son. Moltmann speaks of a "death *in* God".[12] Yet in this absolute and terrible separation of Father and Son there is, through the Spirit, a unity of purpose.[13] The resurrection prefigures the eschatological unity of God in glory. "The resurrection of the Son abandoned by the Father unites God with God in the most intimate fellowship."[14]

---

10. Jürgen Moltmann, *The Future of Creation* (SCM, 1979), p. 74.
11. Jürgen Moltmann, *The Crucified God* (SCM, 1974), p. 152.
12. Jürgen Moltmann, *The Crucified God*, p. 207.
13. Jürgen Moltmann, *The Spirit of Life* (SCM, 1992), pp. 63–64.
14. Jürgen Moltmann, *The Crucified God*, p. 152.

Through the event of the cross and resurrection, however, this unity is now open to the world. "The Trinity in the glorification is open for the gathering and uniting of men and creation in God."[15] In taking upon himself the godforsakenness, suffering and death of the world, the Son unites the world to God. Christ's death is a death "for us". Even the protest of suffering humanity against God, heard on the lips of the Son of God as he cries "My God, why have you forsaken me?" now exists in God. Moltmann rejects the classical belief that God cannot suffer (God's "impassibility"). This doctrine was built, argues Moltmann, on a false dichotomy between impassibility, and unwilling suffering. In fact God in his freedom chooses to suffer and change.

Like Barth and Rahner, Moltmann complains about the way Western theology has started with the one God before moving on to his threeness. Moltmann looks at the history of Jesus from a trinitarian perspective, examining the involvement of each of the persons of the Trinity at the different stages in that history. For Moltmann God's threeness is a presupposition for an examination of God's unity and not vice versa. Given this, we must "dispense" with one substance and speak of God's "united-ness".[16] The unity of the Trinity, says Moltmann, is an act of will rather than belonging to God's being. It is expressed as community rather than one nature.[17]

So "God" consists of the unity of the three persons, but this unity has a history – the history of sending, cross, resurrection and glorification. As such Moltmann prefers to speak of "the trinitarian history of God" rather than the Trinity. Like Rahner, Moltmann believes the immanent and economic Trinity merge into one another. But

---

15. Jürgen Moltmann, *The Future of Creation*, p. 91.
16. Jürgen Moltmann, *The Trinity and the Kingdom of God* (SCM, 1981), p. 150.
17. Jürgen Moltmann, *The Crucified God*, pp. 243–244 and *The Church in the Power of the Spirit* (SCM, 1977), p. 62.

Moltmann goes further. Reversing the traditional order, Moltmann speaks of the immanent Trinity as the *goal* of the trinitarian history of God. Although Moltmann can say that "the divine relationship to the world is primarily determined by that inner relationship,"[18] the dominant note in his theology is that the economic Trinity completes itself in the immanent Trinity when the history of salvation is completed. What this actually means is not always clear and Moltmann has been criticised for subjecting God to an Hegelian dialectical process.[19]

Moltmann describes the Trinity in terms of perichoresis: the persons of the Trinity are alive in and through one another.[20] And for Moltmann this has social consequences. A number of modern theologians such as Don Cupitt have argued that the traditional doctrine of God is the enemy of human freedom. So Cupitt rejects God as an objective reality. But Moltmann – along with the Catholic theologian, Walter Kasper[21] – argues that, far from upholding monarchy and patriarchy, the doctrine of the Trinity undermines them: "What is normative for all relations in creation is not the structure of command and obedience within the Trinity but the eternal perichoresis of the triunity." This also has ecological consequences. Moltmann speaks of "a perichoretic doctrine of creation":[22] "The triune God is community...and makes himself the model for a just and liveable community in the world of nature and human beings."[23]

---

18. Jürgen Moltmann, *The Trinity and the Kingdom of God*, p. 161.
19. John Thompson, *Modern Trinitarian Perspectives* (OUP, 1994), p. 34.
20. Jürgen Moltmann, *The Trinity and the Kingdom of God*, pp. 174–176.
21. Walter Kasper, *The God of Jesus Christ* (SCM, 1982).
22. Jürgen Moltmann, *History and the Triune God* (SCM, 1991), p. 127; see also *God in Creation: An Ecological Doctrine of Creation* (SCM, 1985), pp. 16–17.
23. Jürgen Moltmann, *History and the Triune God*, pp. xii–xiii.

## Liberation theology: A trinitarian vision of equality

Leonardo Boff (b. 1938), an advocate of liberation theology, also takes up the idea of perichoresis to develop a vision for human community, acknowledging his debt to Moltmann. Boff argues that the eternal divine community is the prototype for all human communities from family to church to nation. The Trinity provides us with a vision for a just society of equals instead of our current exploitative patterns of social interaction. He speaks of the Father as the origin of all liberation, the Son as the mediator of divine liberation and the Spirit as the driving force of liberation.

---

### Liberation theology

Liberation theology first came to prominence in Latin America in the 1970s as a response to poverty and injustice. Liberation theology believes poverty does not arise from a lack of development or education, but from structural injustice. It argues that salvation has a political dimension, indeed some see salvation as primarily political in nature. A key theme for liberation theology is the exodus, which is seen as a paradigm for liberation and God's preferential option for the poor. It has influenced feminist and black theologies.

---

## Feminist theology: A non-patriarchal understanding of the Trinity

Moltmann's concern to develop a non-patriarchal understanding of the Trinity is mirrored in the approach of feminist theologians. Some have tried to coin non-gendered language for the Trinity, speaking of Creator, Redeemer and Sustainer. The problem is that these terms refer to activities of God in which all three persons of the Trinity are involved. Whatever the intentions of its advocates, it suggests a modalistic view of God. Elizabeth Johnson goes further, developing the idea of wisdom (*sophia*) personified. She speaks of God as "SHE WHO IS": Spirit-Sophia, Jesus-Sophia and Mother-Sophia.

Catherine Mowry LaCugna (1953–1997), a Roman Catholic theologian, takes a different approach. She criticises the tendency towards an abstract understanding of the Trinity that is separated from everyday Christian living. She calls this "the defeat of the doctrine of the Trinity". The doctrine of the Trinity tells the story of God's involvement with humanity and affirms that he is relational. We learn from the Trinity, she argues, that persons are persons because they have relationships. So the Trinity provides a vision of "human community structured by relationships of equality and mutuality rather than hierarchy".[24]

### Eastern Orthodoxy: Divine communion

The rise of communism in the twentieth century led to the emigration of a number of theologians from the Eastern Orthodox tradition, especially from Russia. This has resulted in the most creative period of interaction between the Eastern and Western traditions since the fall of the Byzantine Empire. Vladimir Lossky (1903–1958), for example, came from Russia to Paris in 1922. Lossky argues that the modern notion of personhood is not a departure from what personhood means in the Trinity, but the *result* of trinitarian doctrine. Trinitarian doctrine has made significant contributions to humanity's understanding of what it means to be human. John Zizioulas (b. 1931) takes up this idea. He argues that *being* has no meaning apart from persons. He talks about "being as communion".[25] God's identity consists in the communion

---

24. Cited in Philip W. Butin, *The Trinity*, pp. 71–72.
25. John D. Zizioulas, *Being As Communion: Studies in Personhood and the Church* (St Vladimir's Seminary Press, 1985).

of the three persons. As Colin Gunton puts it: "There is no 'being' of God other than this dynamic of persons in relation."[26] In the same way, human identity consists in the communion of persons, for we are made in God's image. This approach has had considerable influence on those in the Western tradition like Moltmann who have developed the communal implications of a social model of the Trinity.

Over the past three chapters we have looked at how the doctrine of the Trinity has developed as people reflected on the biblical data. We have seen how some people thought the Trinity was peripheral while others made it central. We have seen different ways of accounting for the relationship between the Three and the One. We have seen some people shaped by their cultures, and others using the Trinity to engage with their culture. You may like to reflect on which thinkers you are drawn to. What influences and presuppositions, both personal and social, draw you to some understandings of the Trinity and not others?

Theology is a continuing project. We need to re-articulate the gospel afresh to our culture. At the same time we need to examine the influence of our culture on our thinking. The development of the doctrine of the Trinity illustrates how a slightly divergent view can turn out to be a wrong turning that will eventually lead us away from the biblical gospel. A shift of emphasis in one generation can become a dangerous heresy in the next generation. So theology is a serious task for all Christians. But we need not despair. Our forebears in the faith provide us with a rich resource of understanding. Above all we have in the Bible a firm foundation of truth from God himself. We need to hold in tension a humble recognition of the need continually to reform our theology with a

---

26. Colin Gunton, *The Promise of Trinitarian Theology* (T&T Clark, 1991), p. 10.

confidence in the truth. The way we do this is by affirming the Bible as God's authoritative word of truth. As God's word, it constantly challenges our thinking, and as God's word, it speaks reliably to us today.

# PART THREE

# Practical implications

# Chapter 8

# The Trinity and revelation

*We cannot know the infinite God because we are finite and because we are sinful. But God graciously makes himself known to us. So, while we cannot "study" God, we can know him through a personal relationship. And God can be known personally because he is a Trinity of persons in relationship. God can be known because he has revealed himself in his Son and enables us to recognise this revelation by his Spirit.*

## The unknowable God

Humanity has managed to send space probes to the outer reaches of our solar system and land them on other planets. But a manned mission to Mars looks many years off. Moreover, our solar system represents a tiny fraction of our galaxy and our galaxy is but one of millions. We really know very little about the universe in which we live. How then can we expect to know a being who is infinitely greater than the universe? How can we see the invisible God?

I might know some facts about a distant city I have never visited, but I could not claim to know the city. Still less could I claim to know a person I have never met. At best I might form an impression of them by reading about them or talking with people who do know them. But the invisible God is incomparably more distant than any city on earth. And no one has seen him. He is a being so outside of our sphere of experience that it is difficult to see how we could know anything reliable about him, let alone claim to know him. How can the finite know the infinite?

The theology of the first millennium AD – especially as it developed in the East – said God's essence was unknowable. We can only make negative statements about God: God is *un*changing, *im*movable, *in*finite and so on. Even positive statements should really be seen as negative statements. To say that God is spirit is only to say that he is without a body. The leading theologians of Eastern Orthodoxy during the medieval period were Symeon the New Theologian (949–1022) and Gregory Palamas (c.1296–1359). They both championed a movement known as hesychasm (from the Greek word for "quietness") which involves stilling the passions through constant repetition in prayer combined with synchronised patterns of breathing. Palamas argued that God in his essence is unknowable and uncommunicative, but becomes knowable and communicable through his energies. God could not be known, but his energies could be encountered through prayer.

The theologians in the medieval West were more confident in the ability of humanity to know God. They believed God could be known through natural theology – knowledge of God based on observations of the world. Thomas Aquinas developed his "cosmological" arguments for the existence of God in this way. Everything in the world is in motion or change because something else has moved it. But, argued Aquinas, behind all this movement must be an unmoved Mover. In a similar way, every event has a cause and so, unless there is an infinite chain of causes, there must be a first uncaused Causer. Or again, there must be a source behind values like truth and goodness if these are to be anything other than arbitrary notions. The world reflects intelligent design which suggests a grand designer who has made this world for a purpose. Through such rational arguments Aquinas believed we could establish the existence of God.

This tradition took a new twist in the eighteenth and nineteenth centuries with the Enlightenment's emphasis on human reason. In his book *Christianity as Old as the Creation* (1730), Matthew Tindal sought to establish knowledge of God on the basis of natural theology just as Aquinas had done. But whereas Aquinas worked within the framework of revelation, Tindal thought rational persons no longer needed revelation. We could know God through human reason. The result was not the God of the Bible, but the god of deism – a god who is uninvolved in the world he has made.

The Enlightenment forged the worldview known as modernity. But increasingly our world is becoming postmodern. Modernity confidently thought humanity could come to an agreed understanding of ultimate truth. But our pluralistic societies suggest otherwise. Postmodernism is suspicious of all claims to know absolute truth. The more extreme forms like deconstructionism doubt any absolute truth is out there. But most postmoderns simply doubt anyone can confidently know absolute truth. All such truth claims are inherently coercive; a ruse by the powerful to maintain their power. You may have met this attitude as people accuse Christians of being arrogant for claiming to know *the* truth about God. It is important, however, to recognise that postmodernism has a justified critique of modernity. Human beings are not able to know God or arrive at absolute truth through human reason; still less are they able to agree on truth in this way.

We cannot know God because we are finite creatures and he is the infinite Creator. But the real problem with attempts to know God through human reason or human experience is that our minds are darkened by our sin. The problem is not only our creatureliness. The fool in Psalm 14 who says in his heart "there is no God" is not ignorant. "They are corrupt, their deeds are vile; there is no-one who does good," says the Psalmist. What prevents us knowing God is our rebellion against him. Paul says: "For since the creation of the world God's invisible qualities – his eternal power and divine nature – have been clearly seen, being understood from what has been made, so that men are without excuse" (Romans 1:20). At first sight this seems to suggest we can know God through natural theology. But Paul goes on: "For although they knew God, they neither glorified him as God nor gave thanks to him, but their thinking became futile and their foolish hearts were darkened" (Romans 1:21). The problem is that people "suppress the truth by their wickedness" (Romans 1:18). Stephen Williams argues persuasively that behind the Enlightenment's rejection of revelation was a rejection of the ideas bound up with a Christian understanding of reconciliation: human accountability to God, human sinfulness, judgment and atonement.[1] The underlying issue was not a rejection of the *possibility* of revelation, but a rejection of the *actuality* of revelation. People did not like what God has actually revealed about themselves: that they were sinners, accountable to God, facing his judgment and whose only hope was the atoning work of God's Son.

Our inability to know God because of our sin was recognised by the medieval theologian, Anselm of Canterbury. Anselm is sometimes thought of as a great rationalist. His argument for God's existence appears to work from reason alone. He does not even rely on observation of the world. The argument runs something like this: Let's define God as the greatest conceivable being.

---

1. Stephen N. Williams, *Revelation and Reconciliation: A Window on Modernity* (CUP, 1995).

Whatever God is, he must by definition be the greatest there can be. But if God is the greatest conceivable being then he must exist because if he did not exist it would be possible to conceive of a being who was like our conception of God except with the addition of actually existing. If God does not exist we could conceive of a greater being – one that did exist – which must itself be God. Try it on your friends! It appears rationalistic. But immediately before expounding his ontological argument, Anselm prays:

> I acknowledge, O Lord, with thanksgiving, that thou hast created this thy image in me, so that, remembering thee, I may think of thee, may love thee. But this image is so effaced and worn away by my faults, it is so obscured by the smoke of my sins, that it cannot do what it was made to do, unless thou renew and reform it. I am not trying, O Lord, to penetrate thy loftiness, for I cannot begin to match my understanding with it, but I desire in some measure to understand thy truth, which my heart believes and loves. For I do not seek to understand in order to believe but I believe in order to understand. For this too I believe, that "unless I believe, I shall not understand".[2]

Anselm gives thanks to God that we have been made with the capacity to know God. But that capacity is now ruined by sin. We cannot use our human faculties of either reason or experience to understand God. Anselm's knowledge of God is "obscured by the smoke of my sins". And because of his creatureliness, Anselm cannot "penetrate [God's] loftiness". If we are to know anything of God, God must renew our capacity to know him. Our knowledge of God must be as a result of God's work in us. Knowledge of God must begin with faith. Anselm is not trying to understand so that he can believe. Citing Augustine, he says that he believes in order to understand. The arguments for God's existence only "work" if

---

2. Anselm, *Proslogion*, 1.

they confirm what is already accepted on the basis of faith.

If we are to know God then God himself must make himself known through faith. As Calvin argued, the essence of God is unknowable. God is not a subject that we investigate. He is not like a plant that we can explore under the microscope or an event of history that we can research. He is not susceptible to our intellectual investigation. But God has made himself known through the persons of the Trinity. God is known personally or not at all. God is known as Trinity or not at all.

## The God who is personal

God is a subject, not an object. We use the word "subject" of a topic of enquiry. We study subjects at school. But in grammatical terms the "subject" of a sentence is the person or thing that does the action described in the sentence. In this sense God is not a passive object into which we enquire. God is the "subject" of revelation. He is the one acting. In revelation he acts in history to communicate himself.

Imagine what it must have felt like for the Spanish conquistadors who "discovered" the Incas city of Cuzco – the "city of gold" as they called it. They had travelled halfway round the world, hacked their way through uncharted jungle, encountered numerous threats and dangers. And now they had found what they were looking for: a marvellous civilisation promising fabulous wealth. This is how some people imagine humanity's quest for God. We are like brave explorers, using human reason to cut our way through superstition and myth. Or maybe we are like monks spending our time in mystical contemplation until we arrive at enlightenment. Or maybe knowing God is the reward for a life of good works and religious activity. Whatever the means, knowing God is seen as a noble quest that brings out the best in humanity.

Nothing could be further from the Bible's vision of knowing God. Christians are not those who have searched for and found God. They are those who have been found by God. We may think we have grasped God, but in reality he is the one who takes hold of us (Philippians 3:12). Revelation is not a body of facts, but the actions of God in time and space. Emil Brunner says: "The lordship and love of God can be communicated in no other way than by God's self-giving."[3] We do not ascend to heaven in our thinking to apprehend the mystery of God. God has descended from heaven to make himself known. In Christ God "has communicated not just something about himself but his very Self."[4]

This means that revelation is personal and must be personal. Because God is personal he can enter into personal relationships with us. He can decide to reveal himself to us. He is not some impersonal force that pervades the universe, nor a set of moral principles that earlier generations objectified. He is a personal being with whom we can have a personal relationship. Only in the context of a relationship do we begin to know about him. Revelation still has propositional content because God himself is the One who is truth (see John 14:6–8). God has revealed himself through his Word the Son and we have access to that revelation in God's word the Bible.

God is personal because he exists eternally in the triune relationship. Personhood is about relationships and reciprocity. God cannot be solitary. If the one God is not a community of persons then he cannot be personal and

---

3. Cited in Alister McGrath, *Christian Theology: An Introduction* (Blackwell, 3rd ed., 2001), p. 205.
4. T. F. Torrance, *The Trinitarian Faith* (T&T Clark, 1988), p. 6.

if he is not personal then we cannot know him. God is knowable because he is relational and he is relational because he exists as three persons in relationship. If God were not three persons then he would forever be hidden in "light inaccessible". We have no access to the One except through the Three.

## The God who is revelation

The Trinity has often been seen as a doctrine that synthesises several other fundamental Christian truths: the humanity and divinity of Christ, the indwelling of the Spirit and so on. The Trinity completes and safeguards these prior truths. But, as we saw in the previous chapter, Karl Barth turned this around. Barth made the Trinity the starting point for theology. The Trinity is the precondition for the revelation upon which all theology is built. Barth admits that "in putting the doctrine of the Trinity at the head of all dogmatics we are adopting a very isolated position from the standpoint of dogmatic history."[5]

For Barth the word of God says "No" to all human-centred religion. Instead of starting with humanity, Barth says the starting point for theology is the *fact* of revelation. And we cannot have a true doctrine of revelation without the Trinity. "God reveals Himself. He reveals Himself *through Himself*. He reveals *Himself*."[6] If God were anything other than trinitarian, argues Barth, he would be unknowable. There would always be a God-as-he-is behind the revelation of God unless the revelation of God *is* God both objectively (the Son) and subjectively (the Spirit). God must not only reveal, he must be his revelation and he must be the reception of that revelation.

"Revelation in the Bible means the self-unveiling,

---

5. Karl Barth, *Church Dogmatics*, 1.1, p. 300.
6. Karl Barth, *Church Dogmatics*, 1.1, p. 296.

imparted to men, of the God who by nature cannot be unveiled to men."[7] By emphasising each of the three sections of this statement Barth expounds the Trinity in terms of Revealer, Revelation and Revealedness. The Son is the Revelation or "self-unveiling" of God. The Father is the Revealer – the invisible God "who by nature cannot be unveiled to men". And the Spirit is the Revealedness of God through whom the Revelation of God is "imparted to men".

The Son as the Revelation of God is the objective side of the process of revelation. The Spirit as the Revealedness of God is the subjective side. The Spirit enables us to see in the Son a revelation of the Father. Earlier we said that we cannot know God because (1) finite creatures cannot comprehend the infinite and (2) sin has darkened our minds. Barth's argument is that only trinitarian revelation can overcome these problems. The Son as the Revelation of God means that the Father is truly revealed to our finite minds. The Spirit as the Revealedness of God opens our blind eyes to perceive in the Son the truth of God. "Not only the objective but also the subjective element in revelation, not only its actuality but also its potentiality, is the being and action of the self-revealing God alone."[8] As Vern Poythress puts it: "Truth is trinitarian in character. Jesus is the truth. At the same time, he is the truth about God the Father. He is the truth manifested through the power of the Holy Spirit."[9]

Barth locates his discussion of other religions under the role of the Spirit in revelation. Barth says "religion is unbelief" because it is the rejection of revelation in favour of something of our own making.[10] Barth acknowledges that humanity was made with a capacity

---

7. Karl Barth, *Church Dogmatics*, 1.1, p. 315.
8. Karl Barth, *Church Dogmatics*, 1.2, p. 280.
9. Vern S. Poythress, *God-Centred Biblical Interpretation* (P&R, 1999), p. 64.
10. Karl Barth, *Church Dogmatics*, 1.2, p. 299.

to know God, but now we have lost this knowledge of God. Speaking of Paul's declaration of the unknown God at Athens in Acts Chapter 17 Barth says: "Paul tells them: You knew about this, but this God has become an unknown instead of a known God, for now you worship him ignorantly."[11] Revelation can only come through the Spirit, and when revelation comes we recognise that we cannot know God of ourselves. This means that "revelation does not link up with a human religion which is already present and practised. It contradicts it, just as religion previously contradicted revelation."[12] So Barth describes revelation as "the abolition of religion".[13]

Barth has been criticised for basing his trinitarian understanding of revelation on the *structure* or *form* of revelation rather than on the *content* of revelation.[14] It is as if Barth jumps in a stage too early, seizing on the fact of revelation without waiting to hear what is said. But this is pushing Barth further than he wants to go.[15] Moreover the Scriptures indicate a trinitarian structure to revelation. In the Old Testament revelation involves a self-differentiation within the godhead. In Exodus Chapter 33 Moses is told by God: "You cannot see my face, for no-one may see me and live" (Exodus 33:20). But a few verses earlier we are told: "The LORD would speak to Moses face to face, as a man speaks with his friend" (Exodus 33:11). There is a "dimension" of God whose face Moses cannot see and another "dimension" of God with whom Moses speaks face to face.

But it is with the incarnation and the sending of the Spirit that the trinitarian structure of revelation becomes clear. The Son is the revelation of God. John describes

---

11. Karl Barth, *Church Dogmatics*, 1.2, p. 305.
12. Karl Barth, *Church Dogmatics*, 1.2, p. 303.
13. Karl Barth, *Church Dogmatics*, 1.2, p. 297.
14. Emil Brunner, *The Christian Doctrine of God: Dogmatics Volume 1* (Lutterworth, 1949), pp. 236–237.
15. Karl Barth, *Church Dogmatics*, 1.1, pp. 296–297.

Jesus as the "Word"; the Word who "became flesh and made his dwelling among us". "No one has ever seen God, but God the One and [the] Only [Son], who is at the Father's side, has made him known" (John 1:1, 14, 18). Paul says Christ is "the image of the invisible God" (Colossians 1:15). And the writer of Hebrews says that God has spoken "to us by his Son". "The Son," he says, "is the radiance of God's glory and the exact representation of his being" (Hebrews 1:1–3).

And the Spirit is the means by which we appropriate the revelation of God in Christ. "All Scripture is God-breathed," says Paul (2 Timothy 3:16). The Word of God comes on the breath of God. It was the Spirit who enabled the prophets to speak of Christ (1 Peter 1:10–11; 2 Peter 1:21). It is the Spirit who convicts of sin when people do not believe in Jesus (John 16:7–11). And it is the Spirit who speaks the revelation of Christ in our hearts (John 16:12–15).

How then should we respond to our postmodern friends who doubt any claims to know the truth? We can begin by agreeing with them. Human beings cannot confidently arrive at *the* truth. It is beyond the capacity of human beings to know the invisible God. Even what we might know of God through his creation is obscured by our sin. But God has graciously revealed himself through his Son. And he has opened our darkened hearts through the Spirit. Revelation is as much an act of grace as redemption. And revelation cannot be separated from redemption. Revelation involves much more than imparting information. It involves a personal relationship with the holy God. We know God because in Christ God has revealed himself and because in Christ God has reconciled us to himself. This is how Thomas Binney (1798–1874) put it:

Eternal Light! Eternal Light!
How pure the soul must be,
when, placed within thy searching sight,
it shrinks not, but with calm delight
can live and look on thee.

The spirits who surround Thy throne
may bear the burning bliss;
but that is surely theirs alone,
since they have never, never known
a fallen world like this.

O how shall I, whose native sphere
is dark, whose mind is dim,
before the Ineffable appear
and on my naked spirit bear
the uncreated beam?

There is a way for man to rise
to that sublime abode:
an offering and a sacrifice,
a Holy Spirit's energies,
an Advocate with God.

These, these prepare us for the sight
of holiness above;
the sons of ignorance and night
can dwell in the eternal light,
through the eternal love.

# Chapter 9

# The Trinity and salvation

*Christ's death on the cross can be seen as his victory over Satan and as a moral example. These approaches see salvation as a transaction between God and Satan and between God and humanity. But at its heart salvation is a transaction within the Trinity. The Son offers himself to the Father as our substitute. God both judges and is judged. And the Spirit applies this transaction to our lives.*

I am guessing here, but I suspect that not many people reading this book are all that interested in the load-bearing capacity of steel cable. Just outside of Matlock in Derbyshire, near where I live, is a cable car that takes people up to the scenic "Heights of Abraham". Halfway up, the cable car stops so that people can take pictures. I suffer somewhat from vertigo, so swaying in the wind in a stationary cable car was not a happy experience. Suddenly the load-bearing capacity of steel cable seemed the most important subject in the world – the sort of thing that could save your life.

It is the same with the doctrine of the Trinity. The Nicene Creed confessed that Jesus "for us men and our salvation, came down from heaven and was incarnate by the Holy Spirit of the Virgin Mary, and was made man". The one who is "very God of very God" was made man and the reason was "for us men and our salvation". The issue at stake in their affirmation of the true divinity and humanity of Jesus was "our salvation". As the early church fathers worked out and defended the doctrine of the Trinity in the early centuries after Christ, it was not some esoteric exercise, nor merely a detached affirmation of orthodoxy. At stake was "our salvation".

The Council of Nicaea said the Son was *homoousios* ("the same substance") with the Father. But after the Council the term was widely dropped in favour of a compromise term *homoiousios* ("of a similar substance"). Athanasius stood almost alone against this move. Eventually he won the day, but not until he had endured five periods of exile totalling 17 years. Do the intricacies of theology matter that much? Can you imagine someone today being exiled over one Greek letter? It matters, argued Athanasius, because our doctrine of the Trinity is crucial to a proper understanding of salvation: "No one else but the Saviour himself, who in the beginning made everything out of nothing, could bring the corrupted to incorruption; no one else but the Image of the Father could recreate men in God's image; no one else but our Lord Jesus Christ, who is Life itself, could make the mortal immortal…"[1] The focus may be on the doctrine of God, but for Athanasius the doctrine of salvation is never far away.

## The dramatic view of the atonement

The word "atonement" means reconciliation. It is the term used to describe how the cross of Christ achieved our salvation. The early church fathers saw the cross primarily in terms of Christ's victory over Satan. On the cross Christ liberated us from Satan's power into God's kingdom. It is known as the dramatic view of the atonement because it views the cross as the centrepiece of a great drama. This view was a strong feature of Martin Luther's

---

1. Athanasius, *On the Incarnation of the Word*, 4.20.

thought and continues to hold a dominant place in the theology of Eastern Orthodoxy.

The idea is found in C. S. Lewis' famous allegorical work for children, *The Lion, the Witch and the Wardrobe*. There the white witch, who represents Satan, claims the life of the lion, Aslan, who represents Jesus. Lewis employs substitutionary imagery, for Aslan dies in the place of Edmund, the treacherous son of Adam. But Lewis also speaks in terms of victory and even of trickery. The white witch claims the life of Edmund because of a "deep magic from the dawn of time" which means "every traitor belongs to me as my lawful prey and that for every treachery I have a right to a kill."[2] And so Aslan offers himself in Edmund's place and the witch thinks she has triumphed. But she does not realise that a "deeper magic from before the dawn of time" also operates in the universe. "When a willing victim who had committed no treachery was killed in a traitor's stead...death itself would start working backwards."[3] The death of Aslan means defeat for the white witch. She thinks that through Aslan's death she has triumphed. But in fact through his death she is defeated. She is tricked, her power is broken and Aslan is victorious.

In the discussion of the cross by the Greek church fathers the idea of ransom was a dominant motif (see Mark 10:45; 1 Timothy 2:6). It captures the sense of liberation that is achieved through the cross and the idea of Christ's blood as a payment for our sin (1 Peter 1:18–19). More problematic was the question of to whom the ransom was paid. It could not have been paid to God because God did not hold sinners ransom, argued Origen, so it must be a payment made to Satan. Gregory of Nyssa took up this idea, arguing that through the fall Satan

---

2. C. S. Lewis, *The Lion, the Witch and the Wardrobe* (Collins, 1950, 1988), p. 128.
3. C. S. Lewis, *The Lion, the Witch and the Wardrobe*, p. 148.

had acquired rights over humanity. The only way that God could rightfully release humanity was if Satan exceeded his legitimate rights. Gregory believed that Jesus the sinless one took the form of sinful humanity so that Satan was tricked into wrongfully claiming Jesus' life and so overstepping his rightful authority. He used the image of a baited hook. Christ's humanity was the bait; his divinity the hook. In medieval times the idea of victory over Satan was portrayed in the image of the "harrowing of hell". Using 1 Peter 3:18–22, it was argued that at his death Christ descended to hell forcibly to release its imprisoned souls.

The medieval theologian, Anselm, objected to the idea of a ransom being paid to Satan. He could not accept that Satan had legitimate rights over humanity. Satan may have power over humanity, but this is not a legitimate authority which God is obliged to respect. Moreover, he could not accept that God employed trickery or deceit. God must act righteously. Indeed for Anselm atonement is the means by which God *maintains* his righteousness in the salvation of humanity. To this critique we might add the observation that, while the New Testament does use the language of ransom and redemption, it does not do so in relation to the devil. The language of ransom is limited. It expresses the fact that we are slaves set free by the blood of Jesus. But, as John Stott says, "The New Testament never presses the imagery [of redemption] to the point of indicating to whom the ransom was paid."[4]

In more recent times the dramatic view of the atonement has been re-emphasised. The Swedish theologian, Gustav Aulén (1879–1977), wrote an influential book entitled *Christus Victor* ("Christ the Victor"). Aulén did not think the ransom was paid to the devil, but he did want

---

4. John Stott, *The Cross of Christ* in *The Essential John Stott* (IVP, 1999), p. 164.

to rehabilitate the view of the atonement as a victory over Satan. He called this approach the "classic" view of the atonement because, he argued, it had been the dominant model throughout the first millennium. Aulén's work came at a time when other approaches to the atonement were being questioned, and coincided with a post-Freudian renewal of interest in the forces that bind human beings. Paul Tillich reworked Aulén's ideas, seeing the cross as victory over the forces which threaten authentic human existence. Paul Fiddes writes: "The victory of Christ actually creates victory in us... The act of Christ is one of those moments in human history that 'opens up new possibilities of existence'. Once a new possibility has been disclosed, other people can make it their own, repeating and reliving the experience."[5]

## The satisfaction or substitutionary view of the atonement

The satisfaction view of the atonement was first presented in developed manner by the aforementioned Anselm (c.1033–1109). A Norman monk, Anselm was made Archbishop of Canterbury in 1083, but spent much of his time as Archbishop in exile because he insisted on the independence of the church from the king. In exile he wrote *Cur Deus Homo* (*Why God Became Man*) in the form of dialogue between Anselm and Boso, one of his monks.

Sin, argues Anselm, is "not rendering to God what is his due". We dishonour God by failing to meet our obligation of complete obedience to him. As a result we owe God a debt of honour which requires satisfaction. It is not fitting for this situation to be disregarded. God's honour must be restored. No punishment would mean there was

---

5. Paul Fiddes, *Past Event and Present Salvation* (DLT, 1989), cited in Alister McGrath, *Christian Theology: An Introduction* (Blackwell, 3rd ed., 2001), p. 419.

no difference between guilt and innocence. And a just God must uphold what is right. No mercy is conceivable which involves God acting contrary to his character. This means there are only two alternatives: either suitable satisfaction must be offered to God or God must punish those who have dishonoured him. The alternatives of satisfaction and punishment "hold their own place in the orderly beauty in the same universe".[6]

But humanity can do nothing to repay the debt of honour we owe to God. We owe God everything so anything we could do is part of what we already owe him. We can never catch up on our repayments, as it were. One of the strengths of Anselm's approach is that he takes sin seriously. He talks about "the weight of sin".[7] The failure to understand the necessity of the cross stems from a failure to appreciate the deadly seriousness of humanity's sin. We cannot make satisfaction. But, argues Anselm, the alternative of punishment is also not fitting, for this would thwart God's purposes in creation. Anselm argues that the salvation of humanity is needed to make up the number of fallen angels so that Satan does not have the ultimate victory. This line of argument is not convincing. It is better to say that God does not need to save us, but chooses to do so because of his mercy and grace. If there is a necessity, it is the internal necessity of God's own gracious character. But the dilemma is there all the same: How can God reconcile his mercy and his justice without denying either? We owe God the world, so what could we give to repay our debt? The only thing greater than the world is God himself. Only God can make satisfaction. But only man owes satisfaction. It is, therefore, necessary to have the God-man.

Anselm went on to argue that, while life is owed to

6. Anselm, *Cur Deus Homo*, 1.15.
7. Anselm, *Cur Deus Homo*, 1.21.

God, death is only owed when God punishes. Death is not owed to God if a life has been obedient. Voluntary death can thus act as a means of satisfaction. Christ owed God a life of perfect obedience – which he duly delivered. But Christ did not owe God his death. So Christ's death earns a reward. But Christ is the God-man who already has everything. It is, therefore, fitting that his merit should be given to others to pay the debt they cannot repay. Christ's person is of infinite value. His death, therefore, has infinite power to satisfy. Christ makes satisfaction by giving to God the one thing greater than the world – God himself.

*Cur Deus Homo* is open to critique. The picture of God that Anselm presents reflects the feudalism of his day. The focus is on honour and satisfaction. Anselm does not focus on the wrath of God. Instead, Anselm presents satisfaction and punishment as alternatives. But the Bible presents the atonement as involving punishment. Christ bore our punishment. "He was pierced for our transgressions, he was crushed for our iniquities; the punishment that brought us peace was upon him..." (Isaiah 53:5). The Bible talks of "propitiation" which means "turning aside wrath" (Romans 3:24–25; 1 John 2:1–2; 4:10). Opponents of propitiation caricature it by saying that an angry God must be made loving by the death of a victim. But in Christian theology it is God himself who makes propitiation. The Father presents Jesus as the propitiating sacrifice. Jesus offers himself in our place, turning aside God's wrath through his death. He, as it were, interposed himself between us and the holy wrath of God.

These weaknesses in Anselm's position led the Reformed tradition to develop a substitutionary or penal substitution model of atonement from Anselm's ideas. Substitutionary atonement is the belief that Christ was our substitute – he died our death and bore our judgment instead of us. Penal substitution was another way of expressing this. "Penal" comes from the word "penalty". Christ bore the penalty of our sin.

> At the cross in holy love God through Christ paid the full penalty of our disobedience himself. He bore the judgment we deserve in order to bring us the forgiveness we do not deserve. On the cross divine mercy and justice were equally expressed and eternally reconciled. God's holy love was "satisfied" ... How then could God express simultaneously his holiness in judgment and his love in pardon? Only by providing a divine substitute for the sinner, so that the substitute would receive the judgment and the sinner the pardon ... The only way for God's holy love to be satisfied is for his holiness to be directed in judgment upon his appointed substitute, in order that his love may be directed towards us in forgiveness. The substitute bears the penalty, that we sinners may receive the pardon.[8]

A family in the Australian outback saw a bush fire swept along by the wind at a terrific speed, coming towards them faster than they could escape. If they were to flee they would be overtaken and consumed. So they lit another fire. Soon the wind caught their fire and drove it along in front of them. They were able to walk along in the scorched earth it had left behind. When the main fire caught up with them it raged all around them, but they were safe in the wake of the fire they had lit. In the same way on the cross God lit the fires of his judgment and Jesus took them on himself. And now we can walk behind him. The fires of God's judgment are coming. One day they will overtake humanity and consume us. But those who are in Christ will be safe. The fire of God's judgment will burn around us, but we will be secure in the refuge that Jesus provides. Jim Packer says: "Penal substitution is the notion that Jesus Christ our Lord, moved by a love that was determined to do everything necessary to save

---

8. John Stott, *The Cross of Christ*, pp. 84–85, 126, 146.

us, endured and exhausted the destructive divine judgment for which we were otherwise inescapably destined, and so won us forgiveness, adoption and glory."[9]

## The exemplary view of the atonement

Anselm's approach was challenged by Abelard (1079–1142). Abelard had a colourful life. He was educated in Paris, but often set himself up as a rival to his teachers. He lodged with a canon of Notre Dame cathedral called Fulbert and tutored Fulbert's beautiful niece, Héloïse. They fell in love and Héloïse became pregnant and was sent to a nunnery. Abelard was banished and eventually castrated. Their letters remain part of the world's great love literature.

Abelard's criticism of Anselm is that his approach lacks love. The God who has revealed his love in the cross, argues Abelard, does not need a debt to be paid before he forgives. God in his love is already willing to cancel our debt. Instead, the love of God seen in the cross awakens in us a response of love. Sometimes Abelard does use the language of Christ bearing our punishment so it is not clear whether Abelard is simply adding to a satisfaction view of the atonement. What is distinctive is his emphasis on the subjective impact of the cross. In the dramatic and substitutionary views, atonement is an objective work – it achieves a change outside of us which is for us. In Abelard's exemplary view the atonement achieves its work within us – it changes us.

---

9. J. I. Packer, "What did the Cross Achieve? The Logic of Penal Substitution", *Tyndale Bulletin* 25 (1974), p. 25.

## Salvation and the Trinity

The dramatic and exemplary approaches to the atonement are both true. The New Testament clearly portrays the cross of Christ both as victory over Satan and as a moral example. The New Testament repeatedly presents the cross as the standard and guide for Christian discipleship (Mark 8:34; 1 John 3:16–17). The hymn "When I survey the wondrous cross" is testimony to the emotional force of Christ's death upon the sincere believer. But both the dramatic and exemplary approaches to the atonement are rooted in the idea of substitution.

The question that must be asked of the dramatic approach to the atonement is: How was the victory over Satan won on the cross? The passage that most explicitly links the cross to Satan's defeat is Colossians 2:13–15:

> When you were dead in your sins and in the uncircumcision of your sinful nature, God made you alive with Christ. He forgave us all our sins, having cancelled the written code, with its regulations, that was against us and that stood opposed to us; he took it away, nailing it to the cross. And having disarmed the powers and authorities, he made a public spectacle of them, triumphing over them by the cross.

The rulers and authorities are defeated because they have been "disarmed". Satan is the accuser whose weapon is our sin – its control over our lives and the legal demands of the judgment it entails. But now that weapon is rendered powerless, for our sin has been forgiven and we have been given new life. And this liberating forgiveness took place as the record of our debt was nailed to the cross of Christ. The legal demands of sin were placed on Christ in our place. It was this act of substitution that disarmed Satan and led to Christ's triumph over the powers of evil.[10]

---

10. John Stott, *The Cross of Christ*, pp. 216–218.

The same sort of argument can be applied to the exemplary view. If the cross does not effect an objective change, then it becomes an empty gesture. Substitution need not in any way diminish the exemplary nature of the cross. "This is love," says John, "not that we loved God, but that he loved us and sent his Son as an atoning sacrifice for our sins" (1 John 4:10). Gerald Bray argues that those like Abelard who believe God can simply forgive sin without exacting any penalty for that sin "have never really encountered the depths of the love of God in Christ... Unless we understand that we are fully deserving of God's wrath, which he will certainly inflict on those who do evil, we shall never even begin to understand the depth of love which has rescued us from our misery and from our just desserts. It is impossible to have any understanding of the love of God apart from the message of the atoning power of the cross of Christ."[11]

We should not reject the moral influence view of atonement or the dramatic view of atonement. But both these truths rest on the substitution of Christ in our place, bearing our punishment and satisfying God's justice. "Penal substitution is not, as some suggest, one illustrative model among a number from which we can choose those we like best. It is the *primary model* on which all the others depend."[12]

The dramatic and the exemplary views are rooted in the substitutionary view because the substitutionary view is the truly trinitarian view. The classic view presents the atonement as a transaction between God and the devil. Even if a ransom is not paid to Satan, atonement is still seen as an event between God and Satan. In the exemplary view atonement is a transaction between God and humanity. But in the substitutionary view, atonement is

---

11. Gerald Bray, *The Doctrine of God* (IVP, 1993), p. 222.
12. Mark Meynell, *Cross-Examined: The Life-Changing Power of the Death of Jesus* (IVP, 2001), p. 108.

a transaction between God and God; between the Father and the Son through the Spirit. It is an event *within* God. Salvation starts with God, is achieved by God and is applied by God.

Whatever may be the deficiencies of Anselm's understanding of the atonement, this was his great breakthrough: to recognise that atonement was a work within God among the persons of God. "Anselm understood, in a way that many of his predecessors had not," says Gerald Bray, "that Christ's work of atonement on the cross was a work of God *within the Trinity*. It was the Son who offered himself as a sacrifice to the Father, and it is the Holy Spirit who now makes that sacrifice effective in the life of the Christian."[13] This means that atonement is inescapably trinitarian because the atonement is only comprehensible if God is a Trinity of persons. If God were not a Trinity, who would offer the sacrifice to God? And if God were to offer it, who would receive it? The atonement – Christ's death *for* us – is a transaction that takes place within the Trinity. The Son makes satisfaction for the Father, offering himself as a sacrifice to the Father and taking his wrath in our place. Roger Nicole says:

> The redemptive task was not accomplished by a third party entering the fray between the Father and the sinner, but it was the marvellous expression of the love and grace of the triune God, who in spite of the inexcusable character of man's offence was gracious enough to provide a plan of salvation, to effect himself all that was necessary for the fulfilment of that plan (work of Christ) and to apply himself to the sinner the benefits which were secured by his own work as the incarnate Mediator (work of the Holy Spirit).[14]

13. Gerald Bray, *The Doctrine of God*, p. 192.
14. Roger Nicole, "The Meaning of the Trinity" in Peter Toon and James D. Spiceland (eds), *One God in Trinity* (Samuel Bagster, 1980), p. 8.

Only God can provide satisfaction for our sins. We alike are contaminated by sin and condemned by God. There is no human person – except the God-man – who could step forward to make atonement. Only God, as one who is not condemned in his or her own right, is able to bear the judgment of others. Even if a perfect person could have been found as a substitute for sin, they could only atone through eternally dying and they could not atone for all God's people. There could be no finished work, only perpetual atonement. Only an infinite God could carry the full penalty of the eternal damnation of all who believe. As the Son hung on the cross he said, as it were, to the Father: "Now give my people what this act deserves." Salvation is the Father's attempt to match the self-giving of his Son.

But it is not enough that God dies. God must be forsaken and God must forsake. God must be judged and God must judge. God has died for us and God is satisfied. This could not be true apart from the Trinity. Only the Trinity makes it possible to understand the cross as atonement for our sins.

There is debate about whether the divine nature of Jesus died on the cross or whether it was only the humanity of Jesus that died.[15] If the divine Word of God had ceased to exist, it is argued, then the universe which is sustained by his Word would have collapsed. But this argument employs a false definition of death. In biblical terms death is more than the end of existence. It is an existence without God. And it is precisely this that the Son does endure. He is forsaken by God. The One who dies is the Son of God.

Recently the substitutionary view of the atonement has been attacked by Steve Chalke in his book, *The Lost Message of Jesus*. Chalke calls the idea of penal substitu-

---

15. Wayne Grudem, *Systematic Theology* (Zondervan/IVP, 1994), p. 560.

tion a form of "cosmic child abuse – a vengeful Father, punishing his Son for an offence he has not even committed".[16] There are a number of problems with this caricature of substitution. Chalke says substitution does not reflect God's command not to repay evil with evil. But when you look at that command in its context you discover that the reason we are not to repay evil with evil is that vengeance belongs to God (Romans 12:14–21). We refrain from vengeance not because God does not judge evil, but because he does! So we should not take matters into our own hands. Either God will judge people on the last day (Romans 2:1–16) or he has judged them in Christ on the cross. But the main problem with this view of substitutionary atonement is that it assumes a view of the cross that is not truly trinitarian. It assumes the Father and Son are separate individuals. It is indeed unfair for one individual to punish another for crimes he has not committed. But the Son is not another individual. The divine Father and Son are one – sharing one will, sharing one love, sharing one being. As we saw in Chapter 4, a trinitarian view of the cross prevents us thinking that an unwilling Father is placated by the Son or that an unwilling Son is victimised by the Father. Father and Son have one will and one love. They eternally determined together to save a people through the death of the Son on our behalf. And they share one being. God does not punish another. He punishes himself.

This relationship between the atonement and the Trinity operates in both directions. The Trinity is the foundation of the atonement and the atonement is the ultimate revelation of God's trinitarian character. An exclusive emphasis on the exemplary view of the atonement has tended to go hand in hand with a scepticism towards the Trinity and the divinity of Christ as well as

---

16. Steve Chalke and Alan Mann, *The Lost Message of Jesus* (Zondervan, 2003), p. 182.

towards the wrath of God, original sin and the uniqueness of Christ. Once you abandon a trinitarian understanding of Christ it is difficult to make sense of the cross
except as an ideal to which we should aspire or an
example of the transforming power of self-giving love.

> Pluralism and moral example theology of the atonement go
> together... They are preferred by Christians and non-Christians
> because they appear to fit well with the tolerant, humanistic spirit
> of the age and they avoid the offence of Christ and his cross by
> reducing them to one path of self-salvation. In the end, however,
> this approach is fundamentally non-Christian. It capitulates to
> romantic philosophies and spiritualities that take seriously neither
> the human predicament nor the grace of the cross.[17]

The doctrine of the Trinity protects the gracious character
of God's love. God is not only loving, he *is* love, for he is
an eternal community of loving relationships. When he
loves us he does not do so because some quality in us
draws forth his love. Indeed the opposite is the case: God
loves us despite who we are. "God demonstrates his own
love for us in this: While we were still sinners, Christ died
for us" (Romans 5:8). God is not wrath in the same way
that he is love. His wrath is a response to our sin. But his
love is not a response to us. His love does not depend on
the loveliness of the one he loves. It is an act of pure
grace. He loves because he *is* love, and he is love because
he is an eternal Trinity of persons in loving relationship.

> This is the great truth discovered by Anselm of Canterbury, when
> he wrote that the sacrifice and death of the Son was above all a sac-
> rifice made to the Father, on behalf of sinful human beings. Christ
> is our representative, or Mediator, at the judgment seat of God,
> where his sacrifice remains as our plea for forgiveness. Without the
> love of the Son for the Father, which impelled him to make the sac-
> rifice in the first place, without the corresponding love of the Father

---

17. Roger E. Olsen, *The Mosaic of Christian Belief: Twenty Centuries of Unity and Diversity*
(IVP/Apollos, 2002), p. 253.

for the Son, by which he accepted the Son's work and pronounced the word of forgiveness for us, our salvation could not have occurred. Furthermore, without the love of the Holy Spirit for both the Father and the Son, by which he brings this message to us and sounds the very depths of our hearts, Christ's work of love would have no practical meaning in our lives. The inner love of the persons of the Trinity is the very ground of our redemption, and at the heart of this love we meet both the wrath and the mercy of God.[18]

Imagine a friend comes to you. Sarah has no assurance that her sins are forgiven by God. She feels guilt and shame. Moreover, Sarah was abused by her father as a child and has carried the emotional scars into adulthood. How do you speak to Sarah?

You might tell her that God loves her and point to the cross (the exemplary model of the atonement). But on its own this is little more than a divine arm round the shoulder. It promises forgiveness, but there is no real assurance because the problem of sin is left unresolved. And it does nothing to put things right for Sarah. Indeed it suggests the sins perpetrated against her do not really matter since God can choose to ignore them. A love that ignores justice is not really love.

You could tell Sarah that she is free from her past – she need no longer be plagued by her emotional demons (the dramatic view of the atonement). This may be true, but again it gives her little assurance. She still sins. The fear of God remains. Both the exemplary and dramatic views of the atonement leave God's judgment against sin unresolved. They cannot reconcile God's love and justice.

Some of Sarah's sense of shame is no doubt inappropriate – the result of being victimised by her father. You may need to disentangle false guilt from true guilt. But Sarah is guilty. She is a sinner. We cannot comfort people by minimising their guilt. It does not work because it is

18. Gerald Bray, *The Doctrine of God*, pp. 222–223.

not true. Empty words of reassurance will not console a guilty sinner. But we can fill our words of reassurance with genuine content by pointing to Christ's sacrifice on the cross. The cross does not minimise our sin nor God's anger against it. In fact it is the cross that shows us just how sinful we are and the full extent of God's judgment. We are so sinful that the only solution to our sin was the death of God himself in the person of his Son. But through his death Jesus takes our guilt and bears our punishment. God is seen to be the just God who punishes sin and the loving God who forgives sinners. The trinitarian God judges and is judged. And that offers true hope for Sarah. She can be confident that she will receive justice. God does care for the victims of sin. And she can be confident that she is forgiven. The problem of her sin has not simply been pushed aside so that it still lurks offstage. It has been dealt with finally and completely. God's judgment has not been ignored. He has born it himself in full. God's love for Sarah – for you and me – has real content. "God demonstrates his own love for us in this: While we were still sinners, Christ died for us" (Romans 5:8).

# Chapter 10

# The Trinity and humanity

*We were made in the image of the triune God. We find our identity through relationships. Just as there is both unity and plurality in God, so communal identity should not suppress individual identity and individual identity should not neglect communal identity. Through our union with Christ by faith, Christians are being remade in the image of the triune God. The church should be a community of unity without uniformity and diversity without division.*

Imagine that your church leaders had announced that they would like you to bring your last three bank statements and pay slips to the next church meeting. We are going to talk about each other's financial affairs, they explain, and agree what you should do with your money. How would you react? You may think it is good idea, but I suspect the initial reaction of most Christians would be outrage. "My money is my affair," we might say. "I don't want other people telling me what to do with it. I earned it and I'll decide how I spend it." That is certainly the attitude in our society. We are a society of individuals. Personal freedom and choice is everything. The political discourse is all about individual consumer rights. We do not want to take responsibility for others. Ultimately I am answerable only to myself. But, when others are also answerable only to themselves, the result is fragmentation and isolation.

The life of God is very different.

## God is a triune community

Consider the closing words of Jesus' prayer on the night before he died:

> I pray also for those who will believe in me through their message, [21] that all of them may be one, Father, just as you are in me and I am in you. May they also be in us so that the world may believe that you have sent me. [22] I have given them the glory that you gave me, that they may be one as we are one: [23] I in them and you in me. May they be brought to complete unity to let the world know that you sent me and have loved them even as you have loved me.
>
> [24] Father, I want those you have given me to be with me where I am, and to see my glory, the glory you have given me because you loved me before the creation of the world.
>
> [25] Righteous Father, though the world does not know you, I know you, and they know that you have sent me. [26] I have made you known to them, and will continue to make you known in order that the love you have for me may be in them and that I myself may be in them. (John 17:20–26)

It is as if the camera pans up from the actions of God in history and we are swept up into the eternal being of God. We see for a moment the inner life of God. Three times Jesus speaks of the Father's love for him (vv. 23, 24, 26). Jesus prays that those who trust in his name may "see my glory, the glory you have given me because you loved me before the creation of the world" (v. 24). From all eternity the Trinity has existed in love. God is not a solitary individual, but a divine community. God is persons-in-relationship.

But the Trinity is more than a close family. The persons of the Trinity share one divine nature. It is a community of *being*. In verse 21 Jesus prays that those who will believe in him will be one "just as you [Father] are in me and I am in you". Again in verse 23 he speaks of "you in me". Addressing the Father, he prays that his disciples may be one even "as we are one" (v. 22). Father, Son and

Spirit mutually indwell one another. The Father is *in* the Son. The Son is *in* the Father. To see the Son is to see the Father (John 14:9). "I and the Father are one," says Jesus (John 10:30). The three persons inhabit, as it were, one divine being. As we have seen, the Cappadocian Fathers developed what became known as the idea of perichoresis to express this. Each person of the Trinity shares the life of the other two so in each person the being of the one God is fully manifested. The eternal God-in-himself is a mutually indwelling, loving community.

## We are made in the image of the triune community

In Genesis Chapter 1 God says: "'Let us make man in our image, in our likeness' … So God created man in his own image, in the image of God he created him; male and female he created them" (Genesis 1:26–27). Some people have said that we are made in the image of the one God, often then defining that image in terms of our rationality. Others have suggested we are made in the image of the Son since the Bible talks about Christians being remade in Christ's image. But the text suggests we are made in the image of the Trinity. The passage speaks of God as both one and many. "God created man in *his* own image" – the oneness of God. "Let *us* make man in *our* image" – the plurality of God. Being made in God's image seems to involve ruling over creation under the rule of God. But it also involves sharing God's relationality. We are made for relationships in the image of the one-in-three God. We are made for plurality and unity. "In the image of God he created *him*" – that is our oneness. "Male and female he created *them*" – that is our plurality.

## The one and the many

In the Trinity the one and the many are perfectly integrated. Unity and diversity are perfectly realised. The unity of God does not compromise the diversity of the persons and the diversity of the persons does not compromise the unity of God. And this is how it should be in human society. Humanity is modelled on the triune community. The one and the many should be integrated. God is diverse and we, too, are diverse persons with our own individuality. Yet God is also one and we, too, have communal identities. Human society is neither a unified whole in which the community matters more than individuals, nor loosely connected individuals. Neither a collectivist vision of society, nor an individualist vision reflects our true humanity. Trinitarian Christianity offers a way of being human together that integrates unity and diversity. We are people in community without losing our own personal identities.

But this is not how it is. When humanity rebelled against God in Genesis Chapter 3, Adam, Eve and the serpent formed a triumvirate-in-conflict, passing the blame to one another. Community is broken. And so in Genesis Chapter 4, Cain kills Abel. Human society becomes fractured and fragmented. Ever since we have failed to integrate the one and the many; the communal and the individual.

## The many over the one

Sometimes we particularise so much that diversity becomes division. We see this in individualism. Biblical Christianity gives dignity to the individual as a person made in the image of God and, argues Vinoth Ramachandra, "most forms of political liberalism derive from the traditional Protestant belief in the inherent dignity of the individual and the consequent right of individual conscience." But, he goes on, "by absolutising the individual it turns into a philosophy of individualism: namely, the dogma that I can be myself without my neighbour."[1] As Peter Lewis puts it: "The centre of the universe is getting rather crowded."[2]

At the beginning of the film *About A Boy*,[3] the central character, Will Freeman, says:

> In my opinion all men are islands. And what's more now's the time to be one. This is an island age. A hundred years ago for instance, you had to depend on other people. No-one had TV or CDs or DVDs or videos or home espresso makers. As a matter of fact they didn't have anything cool. Whereas now, you see, you can make yourself a little island paradise. With the right supplies and, more importantly, the right attitude you can be sun-drenched, tropical, a magnet for young Swedish tourists. And I like to think that perhaps I'm that kind of island. I like to think I'm pretty cool. I like to think I'm Ibiza.

This is the creed of individualism. As the film progresses, however, Will learns that it is not true. And the film ends with him celebrating Christmas with an associated group of disparate people who form a community in which he finds belonging and identity.

## The one over the many

In contrast to individualism, sometimes human societies have universalised so that unity becomes uniformity. We see this in totalitarian regimes where the state restricts personal freedoms and constrains individual expression. For totalitarianism and terrorism individual human beings are expendable in pursuit of the cause – "the many" are entirely subservient to "the one".

1. Vinoth Ramachandra, *Gods That Fail: Modern Idolatry and Christian Mission* (Paternoster, 1996), p. 22.
2. Peter Lewis, *The Message of the Living God* (IVP, 2000), p. 293.
3. *About A Boy* (2000), directed by Chris and Paul Weitz with screenplay by Peter Hughes. Based on the novel by Nick Hornby (Penguin, 2000).

Institutionalism is the same: it cannot accommodate diversity. The concerns of individuals can be suppressed to protect the organisation or church.

We see it, too, in more subtle imperialisms. We feel lost in a world where each of us must define ourselves for ourselves, so ironically the by-product of individualism is often a desire for conformity. We see this in the McDonaldisation of the world – the spread of a homogeneous, global culture which destroys or co-opts local cultures. Peter Lewis says: "We are encouraged to express and promote our own self-image, but as everyone else is doing the same it is somehow losing its force, its relevance and even its point. We are losing our uniqueness in the very age that affirms our individuality."[4] Colin Gunton says: "the pressures of modernity are pressures to homogeneity. We might instance the consumer culture with its imposing of social uniformity in the name of choice – a Coca Cola advertisement in every village throughout the world… Modernity is the realm of paradoxes: an era which has sought freedom, and bred totalitarianism."[5] This desire for uniformity is at its most sinister when we allow no space for people who are different: whether they be immigrants living in our community or handicapped children who must be aborted.

### Person-in-relationship
The key to integrating the one and the many is found in a trinitarian understanding of personhood. Because humanity is made in the image of the Trinity, we become truly human the more we image the Trinity. Personhood in the Trinity is not defined in opposition to others, but through relationship with others. "The persons do not

---

4. Peter Lewis, *The Message of the Living God*, p. 293.
5. Colin Gunton, *The One, The Three and the Many: God, Creation and the Culture of Modernity* (CUP, 1993), p. 13.

simply enter into relations with one another, but are constituted by one another in the relations."[6] The Father is the Father because he has a Son and so on. The Father, Son and Spirit are not persons because they operate independently of one another. They are persons in their relationships with one another. Indeed, as we have seen, their personhood is realised in the total interdependency of a perichoretic relationship. God is persons-in-relationship.

Human personality can only be analogous to divine personality. But, made in the image of the Trinity as we are, human personhood is realised through relationships just as divine personhood is. The doctrine of the Trinity shows us that relationships are essential for personhood. A "person" is like a "mother" or a "son". It has no meaning apart from relationships with other people. You cannot be a childless mother, a parentless son or a "relationless" person. What defines a mother is the fact that she has children. What defines a person is the fact they have relationships with other people. Colin Gunton talks about "a doctrine of human perichoresis" in which "persons mutually constitute each other, make each other what they are."[7]

This is the opposite of individualism. Individualism defines individuality as difference. When asked who we are we often answer in terms of our difference from other people. If I dyed my hair red to be different people might say I was "expressing my individuality". Identity is defined by difference. But true identity is found in relationships. I find my identity as the husband of my wife, the father of my two daughters, a member of a Christian community, a child of God.

---

6. Colin Gunton, *The One, The Three and the Many*, p. 214.
7. Colin Gunton, *The One, The Three and the Many*, p. 169.

This means that when we act in a way to diminish those relationships we dehumanise ourselves.

> We need others in order to know who we are and it is from others that we receive our value. When we become a law unto ourselves, when we boast of our self-sufficiency and give ourselves up to a gross and swollen individualism, when we become self-determining, making up our own ethic and standards, careless of what others think of us or expect from us, then it is that we begin to lose ourselves.[8]

If we pursue fulfilment in our career to the detriment of our children, we do not realise our individuality, we dehumanise ourselves. If I choose to divorce because my marriage is not fulfilling my needs as an individual, I dehumanise myself. "This loss of 'independence' [in marriage] is not an impoverishment," says Donald Macleod. "It is an enrichment as we enter upon a life of mutual love and service."[9] If a society organises itself around individual consumer rights alone or diminishes mutual obligations then it impoverishes its members.

This individualism has its seeds in Augustine's focus on the human mind as that which best reflects the image of God within us. A century after Augustine, the Christian philosopher, Boethius, formed what proved to be an influential definition of a person as "an individual substance of rational nature". This comes to fruition in René Descartes' declaration that "I think, therefore I am." A person is a solitary, rational individual. But if what makes me human is my rationality or my rights or any other supposedly universal characteristic of humanity then it is difficult to say what makes me unique. "If you are real and important...as the bearer of some general characteristics, what makes you distinctively you

---

8. Peter Lewis, *The Message of the Living God*, p. 294.
9. Donald Macleod, *Shared Life: The Trinity and the Fellowship of God's People* (Christian Focus, 1994), p. 56.

becomes irrelevant."[10] I am lost in the mass of humanity. But if relationships define my humanity then it is a different story. The matrix of relationships of which I am part are unique to me. The role I play within them defines my distinctiveness. "Everything…is what it uniquely is by virtue of its relation to everything else."[11] But, because I am defined by relationships, this uniqueness does not lead to a solitary, fragmented existence. We find ourselves by being related to others, not by distancing ourselves from them. We find ourselves in giving and receiving. We are neither wholly the active subject of individualism nor the passive object of collectivism. "The heart of human being and action is a relationality whose dynamic is that of gift and reception."[12]

> When marriages and parenthood are deficient in love and its generous self-expression and self-giving, and when our old, sick, handicapped, poor or disadvantaged are ignored and unhelped, then the life of the triune God is not reflected in our humanity as it should be; then personhood itself is wounded and reduced. Where recognition of others, where kindness, gratitude and care are lacking, the person who has left these behind, however successful in other respects, has shrunk not grown in terms of their true personhood. They are diminished, not greatened, in their self-sufficiency.[13]

## We are remade in the image of the triune community

As we participate in Christ through faith so we participate in the divine community. John 17:20–26 is hard to read because the pronouns take you by surprise. "I in them and you in…" says Jesus and we expect him to continue "you in them", but in fact he says "you in me" (v.

---

10. Colin Gunton, *The One, The Three and the Many*, p. 46.
11. Colin Gunton, *The One, The Three and the Many*, p. 173.
12. Colin Gunton, *The One, The Three and the Many*, p. 225.
13. Peter Lewis, *The Message of the Living God*, p. 294.

23). In verse 21 Jesus says to the Father: "you are in me and I am in you." This is the perichoretic life of the Trinity. But in verse 23 Jesus is in the disciples and the Father is in Jesus. Our participation in Christ means participation in the Trinity. We share the trinitarian life. The Father loves us with the same love with which he loves the Son (v. 24). We are part of the family. The Father is our Father. The Son is our brother. The Spirit indwells us.

So the Trinity is to be our *pattern* as we integrate the one and the many. But it is more than a pattern. For Christians it is our life. We *participate* in the trinitarian community through the Holy Spirit. Jesus does not simply say, "May they be *like* us." He says: "May they also be *in* us" (v. 21). Paul Fiddes says we should "complement the *imitation* of God with a thoroughgoing attempt to speak of *participation* in God".[14] The danger of imitation alone is that we lose the mystery of the Trinity and think of it as an image of human community.

We participate in the trinitarian community because we are united to Jesus by the Spirit. Through the Spirit we are in Christ and Christ is in us. This is perhaps the best image of the perichoretic life of the Trinity that we can have. To be indwelt by the Spirit does not mean there is a cavity in our hearts glowing with the presence of the Spirit. The Spirit, as it were, shares the same space as us. And through the Spirit Christ dwells in us.

The church is the new humanity being remade in the image of God. "The manifest inadequacy of the theology of the church," argues Colin Gunton, "derives from the fact that it has never seriously and consistently been rooted in a conception of the being of God as triune." Instead we think of the Trinity as "one of the *difficulties* of Christian belief". But, in neglecting it, we fail to appropriate "its rich store of possibilities for nourishing a gen-

---

14. Paul S. Fiddes, *Participating in God: A Pastoral Doctrine of the Trinity* (DLT, 2000), p. 29.

uine theology of community".[15] In the church we are striving with the Spirit's help to express the plurality and unity of God; to be the one and the many without compromising either. "In Christ we who are many form one body, and each member belongs to all the others" (Romans 12:5).

Viewing God primarily as a monarchy of one will tend towards a hierarchical view of the church. But a trinitarian view of the divine persons in perichoretic relationship will tend towards a communitarian view of the church. "The more a church is characterized by a symmetrical and decentralized distribution of power and by a freely affirmed interaction, the more it will correspond to the trinitarian communion."[16] Empires all have a tendency towards homogenisation. They impose a common culture and deny difference. But in the "empire" of the Lamb there is unity with diversity. People "from every nation, from all tribes and peoples and languages" join together around the throne and before the Lamb (Revelation 7:9–10, ESV).

But evangelicalism tends to face the opposite problem with a lack of commitment to Christian community. We reflect the individualism of our age. We conceive of ourselves primarily as many individuals and then project this back onto God, making him in our image as the God who is many at the expense of his unity. We can conceive of Father, Son and Spirit, but not Father, Son and Spirit as one being. And so our churches function as groups of individuals rather than as one interdependent community. We have reduced the idea of being one in the Spirit to not falling out or institutional collaboration. It is a long way from Paul's language of belonging to one

---

15. Colin Gunton, *The Promise of Trinitarian Theology* (T&T Clark, 1991), pp. 58–59.
16. Miroslav Volf, *After Our Likeness: The Church as the Image of the Trinity* (Eerdmans, 1998), p. 236.

another (Romans 12:5). In Philippians 2:2 Paul talks of "being of the same mind, having the same love, being in full accord and of one mind" (ESV). It could be a description of the Trinity, but in fact it is a description of the Christian community. The church is grounded in our participation in the immanent Trinity through the economic Trinity.

> The church is the human institution which is called in Christ and the Spirit to reflect or echo on earth the communion that God is eternally. The church is therefore called to be a being of persons-in-relation which receives its character as communion by virtue of its relation to God, and so is enabled to reflect something of that being in the world.[17]

In the prayer known as the Grace we talk about "the fellowship of the Holy Spirit" (2 Corinthians 13:14). It is literally "the participation" or "the communion" of the Spirit. The Spirit creates community. Through the reconciling work of Christ, the Spirit brings us together, making us one body. The true Pentecostal church is a community – a community in which people share their lives and possessions with one another (see Acts 2:42–47). The true charismatic church is a community – a community in which there is unity-in-diversity and diversity-in-unity. As Paul describes the charismatic gifts of the Spirit in 1 Corinthians 12 his central point is that in the church there is both unity and diversity: "There are different kinds of gifts, but the same Spirit. There are different kinds of service, but the same Lord. There are different kinds of working, but the same God works all of them in all men" (1 Corinthians 12:4–6). There is one Spirit, one Lord and one God – a clear trinitarian statement. The same Spirit gives gifts to each of us; we serve the same Lord; and the same God works in us. Yet, although there

---

17. Colin Gunton, *The Promise of Trinitarian Theology*, p. 12.

is one Spirit, he gives different types of gifts. Although there is one Lord, there are different ways of serving him. Although there is one God, he works in us in different ways. Our difference is derived from the trinitarian God in grace and offered to the trinitarian God in service. And so, the many gifts are given for one purpose. "To each one the manifestation of the Spirit is given for the common good" (1 Corinthians 12:7). Paul lists a variety of gifts (1 Corinthians 12:8–11). God delights in this variety just as each snowflake that he creates is different. At the same time, for each gift there is one purpose: the common good. If we miss the need for a variety of gifts we will end up with uniformity. If we miss the need to use gifts for the common good we will end up with division.

Paul develops his argument with the image of a body: there is one body made up of many members. It is crazy to think of a body consisting entirely of hands! But it is also crazy to think of a divided body with its members trying to do opposing things. Bodies are united by their head. In the same way Christians are one body with one purpose united by their head – the Lord Jesus. I need to realise that the body needs me so I need not feel inferior (1 Corinthians 12:15–20). Suppose, says Paul, your foot thought that because it could not do the things a hand can, it was not needed. You would soon fall over! In the same way, your gifts are vital. I also need to realise that I need the body so I cannot feel superior (1 Corinthians 12:21–24). Suppose your eye thought that because only it could see it did not need a hand. You would soon be in trouble. The idea is ludicrous.

But it is the same in the body of the church. We need each other. Other people's contributions may not be spectacular, but they are vital. Paul says the weaker parts are in fact indispensable (1 Corinthians 12:22). The Spirit creates community *through* particularity, not by destroying difference. God has brought us together in one body through the reconciling work of Jesus Christ and the indwelling of the Holy Spirit. We are to be a community in which the lowly are honoured and in which we care for one another. Because the many have become one body, we share suffering and honour together (1 Corinthians 12:25–26). Have you ever had a broken leg? It was not just your leg that was incapacitated. Your whole body found it difficult to get around! In the body of Christ the suffering of one person is felt by all. When an athlete wins a race the medal goes round their neck even though it was their legs that did the running. In the body of Christ the joy of one person is felt by all.

A friend was telling me once how he wished he had the gifts of other people in the church. "You're being too individualistic," I replied. I do not know what response he expected from me, but he told me later it certainly was not that response. Instead of envying the gifts of other individuals, I explained, he should rejoice in the gifts of *our* church. In a very real sense, their gifts were his to benefit from.

The Lord's Supper is often called "communion". The word comes from 1 Corinthians 10:16 where Paul asks: "Is not the cup of thanksgiving for which we give thanks a participation [communion] in the blood of Christ? And is not the bread that we break a participation [communion] in the body of Christ?" The wine reminds us that we participate in Christ through faith. The bread reminds us that we participate with one another in the body of Christ. "Because there is one loaf, we, who are many, are one body, for we all partake of the one loaf" (1 Corinthians 10:17).

Yesterday I spoke on the phone to an old friend who is leaving his wife so he can "find" himself. The doctrine of the Trinity is directly relevant to him. The persons of the Trinity are defined by their relationships. They exist in a perfect community of love – neither absorbed into one nor separate from each other. Human beings, made in the image of the triune God, likewise find their identity in relationship with others. We do not "find ourselves" by separating ourselves, but by being in relationship. And so the doctrine of the Trinity speaks to my friend who is leaving his wife. And it speaks to the young student who thinks he can be a Christian without going to church. It speaks to parents who leave their children in nursery all day so they can find fulfilment in their careers. It speaks to the teenage girl who feels trapped by her family. It speaks to the church leader who will not let others take responsibility in the church for fear of losing his authority. It speaks to the family who are only together around the television. It speaks to the young man who will not commit to marriage because he fears losing his precious freedom.

The doctrine of the Trinity is not a stick with which to beat such people. The words it speaks are words of good news – the good news that we can find our humanity in relationship with other people and ultimately in relationship with the relational God.

# Chapter 11

# The Trinity and mission

*The Trinity is a missionary community. The Father sent his Son and his Spirit into the world to redeem his people. So the Trinity is good news. Unlike the god of Islam, the Trinity is relational. Postmodernism fears all truth claims are coercive. But God does not assert his identity against ours, he invites us instead to find true identity by sharing his community. The ultimate apologetic for the Trinity is the Christian community.*

In Chapter 10 we saw how Jesus' prayer in John 17 reveals something of the trinitarian life of God. We saw, too, how we participate in the trinitarian life through our union with Christ. In this chapter we will continue to reflect on John 17, this time looking at its implications for mission.

## The Trinity is a missionary community

The word "mission" comes originally from the doctrine of the Trinity. The word "mission" comes from the Latin word *missio* which means "to send". It was the word Christians used to talk about the sending of the Son and the Spirit into the world. Only in the sixteenth century did Christians start using the term to describe sending people to spread the gospel.[1]

The mission of the church has its roots in the missionary character of the triune God. God is not only God-in-himself (the immanent Trinity). He is also God-for-us

---

1. David J. Bosch, *Transforming Mission: Paradigm Shifts in Theology of Mission* (Orbis, 1991), pp. 227–228.

(the economic Trinity). He has not remained in himself. He has created a world. He has loved his world and he goes on loving his world even after it rejected him. And he came to redeem his world in the person of his Son and through the sending of his Spirit. Three times in John 17:20–26 Jesus speaks of his being sent by the Father (vv. 21, 23, 25). The Son knows the Father (v. 25) and, as he is sent, the Son makes the Father known (v. 26; see also vv. 6–8). The Father has glorified the Son (vv. 22, 24). In John's Gospel the glory of Jesus includes the cross. Jesus is glorified as he is lifted up on the cross, for through the cross he draws people to himself. And through the salvation of his people God is glorified (John 12:28, 31–32).

We experience the Trinity through the sending of the Son and the Spirit. We participate in the Trinity through the glorification of the Son by the Father as we receive eternal life in his name through the Spirit. God is not only relational, he has opened up the trinitarian relations to include us. There is an outward movement of sending and a return movement of glorification.[2] But this twofold movement embraces the world. Peter Toon says: "There is a movement of grace (creation, revelation, salvation) from God toward the world – from the Father through the Son and in/by the Spirit; and there is movement of grace (faith, love, obedience) from the world to God – to the Father through the Son and in/by the Holy Spirit."[3] We see this twofold movement in creation. The Father makes the world through the Word of the Son, a word uttered on the breath of the Spirit. And then creation returns glory to God as the Spirit causes creation to glorify the Father through the mediation of the Son. And we see this twofold movement in salvation. The Apostle

---

2. For a discussion of the implications of this twofold movement for the immanent Trinity see David Coffey, Deus Trinitas: *The Doctrine of the Triune God* (OUP, 1999).
3. Peter Toon, *Our Triune God: A Biblical Portrayal of the Trinity* (Victor Books, 1996), p. 37.

John emphasises the fact that the Father has sent the Son. In the same way the Father sends the Spirit in the name of the Son. Now the Father is glorified as the Spirit causes people to receive eternal life through faith in the Son. Through the Spirit we glorify the Father through the mediation of the Son. The trinitarian community is not exclusive. God opens up the trinitarian community and sweeps us up into it. In verse 24 Jesus anticipates that our participation in God will find eschatological fulfilment as we share in the glory of the triune God.

## The Trinity is good news

"You are in me and I am in you," says Jesus to the Father (v. 21). And this trinitarian identity of God is good news. Colin Gunton believes part of the pathos of Western theology has been its assumption that the Trinity is an obstacle to belief. Too often it has started instead with "some essentially monotheistic natural theology". The resulting remote, unitarian view of god lies behind the crisis of Western Christianity. "The theology of the Trinity," believes Gunton, "…is or could be the centre of Christianity's appeal to the unbeliever, as the good news of a God who enters into free relations of creation and redemption with his world."[4] We have seen how the Trinity is central to our understanding of revelation, salvation and humanity. The Trinity is good news because it means we can know God, be reconciled to God and be truly human. Let us develop these ideas in dialogue with Islam and postmodernism.

### Islam

The central creed of Islam is: "There is no god but Allah and Mohammed is his prophet." The Qur'an explicitly

---

4. Colin Gunton, *The Promise of Trinitarian Theology* (T&T Clark, 1991), p. 7.

rejects the Trinity, caricaturing it as a Trinity of God, Mary and Jesus.[5] It says: "[Allah] is God alone, God the Eternal. He does not beget and He is not begotten. There is none co-equal with Him."[6] To confess this, according to Muslim tradition, is to shed one's sins as a man strips an autumn tree of its leaves.[7] In reality the unity of God has presented problems to Muslim theologians. They have debated whether the attributes of God are eternal. If God is eternally all-knowing then the object of his eternal knowledge must be within himself – suggesting a differentiation within God. A similar debate about the nature of the Qur'an was resolved in the ninth century when Muslim scholars agreed that an uncreated heavenly prototype of the Qur'an has eternally existed.

The unitary God of Islam is remote and unknowable. "In a real sense the Muslim awareness of God is an awareness of the unknown."[8] Islam talks of the *tanzih* (separateness) and *mukhalafah* (otherness) of God. God is utterly removed from us.[9] The Qur'an claims to reveal the will of God, but does not reveal God himself. The word "Islam" means "submission". Although almost every Surah (or chapter) of the Qur'an begins, "In the name of Allah, the Beneficent, the Merciful", Allah's mercy is only his reward of those who submit to his will. There is little sense of God's love and no place for the fatherhood of God.[10] Islam is a religion simply of submission *to* God; not of relationship *with* God. Kenneth Cragg says: "The revelation is conceived of, not as a communication of the Divine Being, but only of the Divine will. It is a revelation, that is, of law not of personality. God the Revealer

---

5. *The Qur'an*, Surahs 4.167–170; 5.77 and 5.116.
6. *The Qur'an*, Surah 112.
7. Kenneth Cragg, *The Call of the Minaret* (OUP, 1956), p. 39.
8. Kenneth Cragg, *The Call of the Minaret*, p. 55.
9. Martin Goldsmith, *Islam and Christian Witness* (OM, 1982), p. 87.
10. S. M. Zwemer, *The Moslem Doctrine of God* (American Tract Society, 1905), pp. 100–102, 110–111.

remains Himself unrevealed... Revelation is not a personal self-disclosure of the Divine."[11] And so Allah does not have relationships with people. The idea that humanity might be made in the image of God – reflecting a relational God and made for a relationship with God – is considered blasphemous in Islam. It is sometimes pointed out that in the Qur'an God is nearer to a person "than his jugular vein". But the context does not suggest an intimate relationship, rather God noting our thoughts and actions for judgment.[12] "Muslims may often feel that God is so distant in his glorious power, that it is unthinkable that we should be able to relate to him in close personal knowledge."[13] In folk Islam this gulf is filled by jinn (spirits), saints and talismans.

Samuel Zwemer, the so-called "apostle to Islam", said "Mohammed's idea of God is out and out deistic. God and the world are in exclusive, external and eternal opposition. Of an entrance of God into the world or of any sort of human fellowship with God he knows nothing."[14] The trinitarian character of the God of the Bible means that the one who is transcendent over creation is also immanent within it. A unitary god must either be separate and distant from creation (a view known as "deism") or it must be one with creation (a view known as "pantheism"). And so it is in Islam. Zwemer again: "Islam is at once deistic and pantheistic. Theologians and philosophers have pantheistic views of Allah, making him the sole force in the universe; but the popular thought of Him is deistic. God stands aloof from creation; only His power is felt."[15]

At the end of the road where we meet as a church is a Sufi centre. The Sufis are a mystical branch of Islam

11. Kenneth Cragg, *The Call of the Minaret*, p. 47.
12. *The Qur'an*, Surah 50.16.
13. Martin Goldsmith, *Islam and Christian Witness*, p. 90.
14. S. M. Zwemer, *The Moslem Doctrine of God*, p. 21.
15. S. M. Zwemer, *The Moslem Doctrine of God*, pp. 69–70.

with strong pantheistic tendencies. In one of their texts, Allah says: "The deepest ground of hell … the highest paradise, the earth and what is therein, the angels and the devils, Spirit and man, Am I … The World Soul Am I."[16] The Sufis, with their emphasis on God's immanence, clash with the majority Sunni Muslims who emphasise God's complete transcendence. "For the Sunni 'ulamā (scholars) the doctrine of God's unicity has ramifications primarily in terms of law. It is not for humans to speculate on the nature of God. Rather it is their duty to obey his commands."[17]

The God of Islam is remote, but the triune God both rules the universe and dwells within us through faith. In Exodus 3:7–8 God hears the plight of his people and promises to "come down". It is a pointer to the incarnation. In Jesus God has come down to dwell among us. Jesus is Immanuel: "God with us". And now he sends his Spirit to dwell within us. The Son is God with us and the Spirit is God in us. God is close. Because God is trinitarian he can be immanent without losing his transcendence and sovereignty. Because he is trinitarian he can reveal himself in his Son and can enable us to receive that revelation through his Spirit.

The God of Islam does not have relationships with people. But we can have a relationship with the triune God because he is himself a relational being. He has existed in trinitarian community throughout eternity. God can love us because the Father has loved the Son and the Son has loved the Father. God made us in the image of the relational God to enjoy a relationship with him. And God has given his Son as an atonement for sin so that relationship can be restored. This is good news: a God who can be known and with whom we can have a

---

16. Cited in S. M. Zwemer, *The Moslem Doctrine of God*, p. 61.
17. Malise Ruthven, *Islam* (OUP, 1997), p. 57.

relationship. Prayer is not a religious duty to perform, but the conversation of friends.

Consider the alternatives to God being eternally tri-une. We could say God does not have personal relationships, in which case we have a capacity (for relationships) that the omnipotent God does not have. Or we could say that God in eternity was only potentially personal, in which case relationships are something God adds to himself, but which are not essentially part of how he is, making God ultimately impersonal. Or we would have to say God needed to create the world to perfect the relational lack in himself. But if God needed to create the world then God's love is not gracious (for God then acts out of his inner need) and creation is not free (for creation would have to meet the divine need). So if God is not eternally triune then "we are left with a lesser God, because we are left with a God for whom personhood is unsatisfied in his essential being before creation." [18]

The undifferentiated God of Islam can create a social vision which does not easily accommodate diversity and difference. According to Malise Ruthven, "if there is a single word that can be taken to represent the primary impulse of Islam, be it theological, political, or sociological, it is *tawhid* – making one, unicity." [19] Medieval Islam was commonly characterised by religious tolerance, with European Jews often finding it more tolerant than medieval Christianity. But today we see another Islam in which the oneness of Allah is being reflected in an oppressive social vision. "I find it hard to see," says Robert Letham, "how Islam, or any religion based on belief in a unitary god, can possibly account for human personality, or explain the *diversity-in-unity* of the world.

18. Michael Ovey, "The Human Identity Crisis: Can We Do Without the Trinity?", *Cambridge Papers* 4:2 (June 1995), p. 3.
19. Malise Ruthven, *Islam*, p. 49.

Is it not surprising that Islamic areas are associated with monolithic and dictatorial political systems?"[20] In such contexts the triune community is good news.

## Postmodernism

In the West, however, we face the opposite extreme. Our postmodern culture is characterised by fragmentation. Our society seems to be losing any sense of unity in the universe. Even the word "universe" is starting to look archaic. It suggests a unified reality. But now we interpret reality as stark plurality. The same is true of the word "university". Universities arose from monasteries. They were called "*uni*versities" because they strove to understand how our diverse world reflects the ultimate truth of its Creator. But this vision has long been lost in the fragmentation and specialisations that characterise modern academic study.

Postmodernism is a reaction to the unitarian tendencies in Western thought. As we have seen, the Western tradition tended towards modalism. In the Enlightenment this runs to seed in Unitarianism. This unitarian vision fed the social unitarianism of state totalitarianism. In other words, a vision in which the ultimate reality is an undifferentiated One creates a social vision marked by oppressive uniformity. Postmodernism is a reaction to this. From oppressive unity we have gone over to fragmented diversity. Postmodernism hears truth claims as coercive. Truth is now a matter of individual choice. Modernity claimed the right for the rational individual to decide what is true. In postmodernism the individual *determines* truth. The result is fragmentation. Truth, beauty and goodness are relative and therefore meaningless. It is not a happy state of affairs.

---

20. Robert Letham, "The Trinity – Yesterday, Today and the Future", *Themelios* 28:1 (Autumn 2002), p. 34.

As we saw in the previous chapter, belief in a triune God means the one and the many are equally ultimate. We can express universal truth without oppressing diversity. Unity and diversity can co-exist. Postmodernism believes all truth claims are inherently coercive; that ultimate truth oppresses diversity. But personhood, as we have seen, is not found in asserting our differences, but in relationship. In the claim of Jesus to be *the* truth, God is not asserting his identity against ours, but inviting us to share his community; to be truly human; to find true identity.

## The Trinity is known through the Christian community

How do we begin to talk about the Trinity? How can we answer people's questions? The best thing to say is probably to start with the story of Jesus. As we see what he did and said we see things which show him to be human, but also things which show him to be divine. Ultimately in the cross we see God differentiated from God, yet uniting us to God.

But what is the apologetic of John 17? Jesus prays:

…that all of them may be one, Father, just as you are in me and I am in you. May they also be in us so that the world may believe that you have sent me. (v. 21)

…that they may be one as we are one: I in them and you in me. May they be brought to complete unity to let the world know that you sent me and have loved them even as you have loved me. (vv. 22–23)

Jesus says the life of the Christian community leads to belief, but specifically this is belief in the Trinity: "you are in me and I am in you." The knowledge of God which people receive through the Christian community is trinitarian knowledge. It is through the unity of God's people – a unity that reflects the oneness of God – that the world will know that Jesus was sent by the Father. For many Muslims the Trinity is the key stumbling block in turning to Christ. Much of the literature on engaging with Muslims focuses on intellectual explanations and defences of the Trinity. But the ultimate apologetic for the Trinity is not some cleverly crafted argument, apposite analogy or philosophical explanation. It is the common life of the Christian community.

The link between Jesus and Yahweh has been a key issue throughout John's Gospel. Now Jesus says the vindication of his claim to be one with the Father will come through the unity of believers. Jesus prays that his followers might be one, participating in the trinitarian life, so that the world will believe. This unity is not institutional. It can be observed and experienced. It is a relational unity that reflects, and participates in, the trinitarian relationships. Nor do we have to be perfect communities, for we witness to the trinitarian mission that unites us to God and to one another through his grace rather than through our goodness. As people see our love for another and our unity in the truth so they confess that Jesus is the truth.

Over the centuries Christians have often tried to come up with an image to explain the Trinity. As we have seen, Augustine spoke of one mind which consists of the distinct, but interrelated entities of memory, understanding and love. Some people point to water which is one substance that can take the form of ice, liquid or steam or to one person playing the different roles of child, spouse, employee. Both of these analogies, however, are closer to modalism than orthodox trinitarianism. Some people see evidence for the Trinity just about wherever they see threes (a three-leafed clover and so on)! But not one of these analogies is satisfactory. They all fall short of a true description of the Trinity. The best such analogies can do is to show that three and one can co-exist. The question is: three what and one what? When we try to answer this through analogies, those analogies lead us astray.

In the second commandment God forbade the Israelites to create an image of him (Exodus 20:4–6). In Deuteronomy Chapter 4 Moses says: "You saw no form of any kind the day the LORD spoke to you at Horeb out of the fire. Therefore watch yourselves very carefully, so that you do not become corrupt and make for yourselves an idol, an image of any shape" (Deuteronomy 4:15–16). When God was revealed at Mount Sinai, the people of Israel "heard the sound of words but saw no form; there was only a voice" (Deuteronomy 4:12). And so the Israelites are not to form anything as a representation of God because God cannot be represented by created things. He is to be without image in the world. Except that Moses continues: "But as for you, the LORD took you and brought you out of the iron-smelting furnace, out of Egypt, to be the people of his inheritance, as you now are" (Deuteronomy 4:20). It is an odd way of describing Egypt – as the iron-smelting furnace. It is the language of making an idol. God himself has cast for himself an image. He has, as it were, poured the people of Israel like molten metal into his own mould. We are not to make any image of God, for God himself has made an image of himself in the world – humanity. God's image in humanity has been marred by our rebellion. But now God's redeemed people are his image in the world. This is how the world will know (see Deuteronomy 4:5–8).

Jesus says that when the world sees our community life they will know that he was sent by the Father to save the world. The challenge is this: When does the world *see* our community life? When do your friends see the love of the Christian community? And would they recognise our community as a work of God and a sign of his grace? Does our community reflect the trinitarian community?

## Conclusion

We began with my two Muslim friends asking me questions about the Trinity. How should I answer those questions?

I would take them to the Gospels and show them the story of Jesus. I would introduce them to the man from Nazareth whose life and words revealed him to be the Son of God sent by the Father. I would take them to the cross and explain how on the cross God both judges and is judged in our place. I would pray that the life-giving Spirit would apply the work of redemption to their lives, opening their eyes to recognise in the Son the revelation of the Father.

But I would also introduce them to the Christian community. I would introduce them to the network of believing relationships of which I am privileged to be part. I would want them to see us participating in the trinitarian life. I would want them to see that we not only submit to God's will, but actually know God as a Father through the Son and by the Spirit. I would want them to see our relationships with one another: not perfect relationships, but relationships that reflect our experience of triune grace. I would want them to see a supernatural community that reflects the sending by the Father of the Son in the power of the Spirit and the glorification by the Spirit through the Son of the Father.

# Further reading

If you want to read something more about the Trinity after reading this book, I suggest Gerald Bray's *The Doctrine of God* or Philip Butin's *The Trinity*. Donald Macleod's *Shared Life* is a good, simple introduction to the doctrine.

## Biblical foundations
Allen Vander Pol, *God in Three Persons*, is a simple introduction to the biblical material starting with the person of Christ. See also Peter Toon's *Our Triune God*; Ben Witherington III and Laura Ice's *The Shadow of the Almighty*; Chapter 1 of Tom Wright's *What Saint Paul Really Said* and Arthur Wainwright's classic, *The Trinity in the New Testament*.

## Historical developments
Many of the works from the Patristic, medieval and Reformation periods are available on the internet. See, for example, www.ccel.org. Most of the key works are published in *The Library of Christian Classics* (Westminster/SCM, 1953–1969). Selections are also available in readers like Alister McGrath (ed.), *The Christian Theology Reader* (Blackwell, 2nd ed. 2001) and Maurice Wiles and Mark Santer, *Documents in Early Christian Thought* (CUP, 1975). The classic history of the doctrine of the Trinity is Edmund Fortman's *The Triune God*. See also Gerald Bray, *The Doctrine of God*; Philip Butin, *The Trinity*; William La Due, *The Trinity Guide to the Trinity* and Ralph Del Colle "The Triune God". On the early church fathers see T. F. Torrance, *The Trinitarian Faith*. Alasdair Heron provides a good introduction to the *filioque* dispute in "The *Filioque*

187

Clause". On the Reformers see Bray's *The Doctrine of God* and Benjamin Warfield, *Calvin and Augustine*. On the modern period see John Thompson, *Modern Trinitarian Perspectives*. Sinclair B. Ferguson and David F. Wright (eds), *New Dictionary of Theology* (IVP, 1988) is also a useful resource.

*Practical implications*

On the Trinity and revelation see Alister McGrath's *Understanding the Trinity* as well as Karl Barth's *Church Dogmatics* (1.1). On different views of atonement see John Stott's classic, *The Cross of Christ*. On the Trinity and humanity see Michael Ovey, "The Human Identity Crisis" and Macleod, *Shared Life*. Harder going, but very stimulating, are Colin Gunton's *The Promise of Trinitarian Theology* and *The One, the Three and the Many*. On the Trinity and the church see Miroslav Volf's *After Our Likeness* which is also summarised in his "Community Formation".

# Select bibliography

Aulén, Gustaf, Christus Victor: *An Historical Study of the Three Main Types of the Idea of the Atonement* (SPCK, 1931)

Barth, Karl, *Church Dogmatics* (T&T Clark, 1960)

Barth, Karl, *Dogmatics in Outline* (SCM, 1949)

Bauckham, Richard, "Biblical Theology and the Problems of Monotheism" in Craig Bartholomew, Mary Healy, Karl Möller and Robin Parry (eds), *Out of Egypt: Biblical Theology and Biblical Interpretation* (Paternoster/Zondervan, 2004/05)

Blyth, Myra, *Celebrating the Trinity* (Grove Books, 2003)

Boff, Leonardo, *Holy Trinity, Perfect Community* (Orbis, 2000)

Boff, Leonardo, *Trinity and Society* (Orbis, 1988)

Bray, Gerald, *The Doctrine of God* (IVP, 1993)

Brown, David, *The Divine Trinity* (Duckworth, 1985)

Brunner, Emil, *The Christian Doctrine of God: Dogmatics Vol. 1* (Lutterworth, 1949)

Butin, Philip W., "Reformed Ecclesiology: Trinitarian Grace According to Calvin", *Studies in Reformed Theology and History* 2:1 (Princeton Theological Seminary, 1994)

Butin, Philip W., *The Trinity* (Geneva Press, 2001)

Calvin, John, *Institutes of the Christian Religion*, The Library of Christian Classics, Vols. XX and XXI (Westminster Press/SCM, 1961)

Chester, Tim, *The Message of Prayer* (IVP, 2003)

Coffey, David, Deus Trinitas: *The Doctrine of the Triune God* (OUP, 1999)

Colle, Ralph Del, "The Triune God" in Colin E. Gunton

(ed.), *The Cambridge Companion to Christian Doctrine* (CUP, 1997), pp. 121–140

Cunningham, David, S., *These Three Are One: The Practice of Trinitarian Theology* (Blackwell, 1998)

Edgar, Brian, *The Message of the Trinity: Life in God* (IVP, 2004)

Fiddes, Paul S., *Participating in God: A Pastoral Doctrine of the Trinity* (DLT, 2000)

Fortman, Edmund J., *The Triune God* (Hutchinson/ Westminster, 1972)

Gunton, Colin E., "The Doctrine of Creation" in Colin E. Gunton, *The Cambridge Companion to Christian Doctrine* (CUP, 1997), pp. 141–157

Gunton, Colin E., *The Christian Faith: An Introduction to Christian Doctrine* (Blackwell, 2002)

Gunton, Colin E., *The One, the Three and the Many: God, Creation and the Culture of Modernity* (CUP, 1993)

Gunton, Colin E., *The Promise of Trinitarian Theology* (T&T Clark, 1991)

Jenson, Michael, "The Very Practical Doctrine of the Trinity", *The Briefing* 249 (March 2001), pp. 11–14

Jenson, Robert W., "The Triune God", in Carl E. Braaten and Robert W. Jenson (eds), *Christian Dogmatics*, Vol. 1, (Fortress, 1984), pp. 83–191

Kasper, Walter, *The God of Jesus Christ* (SCM, 1982)

Kelly, J. N. D., *Early Christian Doctrines*, 2nd ed. (A&C Black, 1960)

La Due, William J., *The Trinity Guide to the Trinity* (Trinity Press, 2003)

Letham, Robert, "The Trinity – Yesterday, Today and the Future", *Themelios* 28:1 (Autumn 2002), pp. 26–36

Lewis, Peter, *The Message of the Living God* (IVP, 2000)

Lonergan, Bernard, *The Way to Nicea: The Dialectical Development of Trinitarian Theology* (DLT, 1976)

Macleod, Donald, *A Faith to Live By* (Mentor, 1998)

Macleod, Donald, *Behold Your God* (Christian Focus, 1990, 2nd ed. 1995)

Macleod, Donald, *Shared Life: The Trinity and the Fellowship of God's People* (Christian Focus, 1994)

McGrath, Alister, "Trinitarian Theology" in Mark A. Noll and Ronald F. Thiemann (eds), *Where Shall My Wond'ring Soul Begin: The Landscape of Evangelical Piety and Thought* (Eerdmans, 2000), pp. 51–60

McGrath, Alister, *Christian Theology: An Introduction*, 3rd ed. (Blackwell, 2001)

McGrath, Alister, *Understanding the Trinity* (Kingsway, 1987)

Moltmann, Jürgen, *History and the Triune God* (SCM, 1991)

Moltmann, Jürgen, *The Crucified God* (SCM, 1974)

Moltmann, Jürgen, *The Future of Creation* (SCM, 1979)

Moltmann, Jürgen, *The Spirit of Life: A Universal Affirmation* (SCM, 1992)

Moltmann, Jürgen, *The Trinity and the Kingdom of God: The Doctrine of God* (SCM, 1981)

Olsen, Roger E., *The Mosaic of Christian Belief: Twenty Centuries of Unity and Diversity* (IVP/Apollos, 2002)

Olyott, Stuart, *The Three Are One* (Evangelical Press, 1979)

Ovey, Michael, "The Human Identity Crisis: Can We Do Without the Trinity?" *Cambridge Papers* 4:2 (June 1995)

Packer, J. I., *Knowing God* (Hodder & Stoughton, 1973)

Parry, Robin, *Worshipping Trinity: Coming Back to the Heart of Worship* (Paternoster, 2005)

Pol, Allen Vander, *God in Three Persons: Biblical Testimony to the Trinity* (P&R, 2001)

Poythress, Vern S., *God-Centred Biblical Interpretation* (P&R, 1999)

Prestige, G. L., *God in Patristic Thought* (Heinemann, 1936)

Rahner, Karl, *The Trinity* (Burns & Oates, 1970)

Ramachandra, Vinoth, *Gods That Fail: Modern Idolatry and Christian Mission* (Paternoster, 1996)

Stott, John, *The Cross of Christ* in John Stott, *The Essential John Stott* (IVP, 1999)

Thompson, John, *Modern Trinitarian Perspectives* (OUP, 1994)

Toon, Peter, *Our Triune God: A Biblical Portrayal of the Trinity* (Victor Books, 1996)

Toon, Peter and James D. Spiceland (eds), *One God in Trinity* (Samuel Bagster, 1980)

Torrance, Alan, "The Trinity" in John Webster (ed.), *The Cambridge Companion to Karl Barth* (CUP, 1997), pp. 72–91

Torrance, James B., *Worship, Community and the Triune God of Grace* (Paternoster/IVP, 1996)

Torrance, T. F., *The Trinitarian Faith* (T&T Clark, 1988)

Torrance, T. F., *Theology in Reconstruction* (SCM, 1965)

Volf, Miroslav, "Community Formation as an Image of the Triune God" in Richard N. Longenecker (ed.), *Community Formation in the Early Church and in the Church Today* (Hendrickson, 2002), pp. 213–237

Volf, Miroslav, *After Our Likeness: The Church as the Image of the Trinity* (Eerdmans, 1998)

Wainwright, Arthur W., *The Trinity in the New Testament* (SPCK, 1962)

Warfield, Benjamin B., *Calvin and Augustine* (P&R, 1956)

Williams, Stephen N., *Revelation and Reconciliation: A Window on Modernity* (CUP, 1995)

Witherington III, Ben and Ice, Laura, *The Shadow of the Almighty: Father, Son and Spirit in Biblical Perspective* (Eerdmans, 2002)

Wright, N. T., *What Saint Paul Really Said* (Lion, 1997)

Wright, N. T., *Who Was Jesus?* (SPCK, 1992)